Understanding the HOLY SPIRIT

With articles by

PERRY B. COTHAM
DON DEFFENBAUGH
BOBBY DUNCAN
WAYNE JACKSON
ROBERT R. TAYLOR, JR.
CLEM THURMAN
FOY E. WALLACE, JR.
GARY WORKMAN

Compiled by

DOROTHY PENSONEAU

Please Return when finished reading

Charleston, AR:
COBB PUBLISHING
2021

There is some excellent material on the gift of the Holy Spirit and His dwelling in the Christian in the book entitled, *What Do You Know About The Holy Spirit?* pages 169-203. We were not able to obtain permission to reproduce those pages from this currently out-of-print book in these notes, but if the reader is able to obtain a copy, he will be blessed by its contents.

Published in the United States of America by:
Cobb Publishing
704 E. Main St.
Charleston, AR 72933
CobbPublishing.com
CobbPublishing@gmail.com
479.747.8372

ISBN: 978-1-947622-82-1

Table of Contents

THE HOLY SPIRIT

Dorothy Pensoneau

The following is a collection of Scriptures relating to the Holy Spirit, showing different aspects of this member of the Godhead.

He is a member of the Godhead

2 Cor. 13:14: The grace of the Lord Jesus Christ, and the love of God, and the communion of the Holy Ghost, be with you all. Amen.

Matt. 28:19: Go ye therefore and teach all nations, baptizing them in the name of the Father, and of the Son, and of the Holy Spirit.

Isaiah 42:8: I am the LORD [Jehovah]: that is my name: and my glory will I not give to another, neither my praise to graven images.

Acts 5:3-4: But Peter said, "Ananias, why has Satan filled thine heart to lie to the Holy Ghost, and to keep part of the price of the land? Whiles it remained, was it not thine own? And after it was sold, was it not in thine own power? Why hast thou conceived this thing in thine heart? Thou hast not lied unto men, but unto God."

Luke 1:67-70: And [John's] father Zacharias was filled with the Holy Ghost, and prophesied, saying, "***Blessed be the Lord God*** of Israel; for he hath visited and redeemed his people, and hath raised up an horn of salvation for us in the house of his servant David; as he spake by the mouth of his holy prophets, which have been since the world began."

2 Peter 1:21: For the prophecy came not in old time by the will of man: but holy men of God spake as they were moved by the Holy Ghost.

In Isaiah 40, John the baptist's preaching mission was foretold.

In Isaiah 41, God's providence is the topic, and he condemns idols and false gods as unable to foretell the future. Only the LORD can truly prophecy future events (verses 22-24). False gods and idols are nothing but wind and confusion (verse 29).

Isaiah 42:5-6: Thus saith God the LORD, he that created the heavens, and stretched them out; he that spread forth the earth, and that which cometh out of it; he that giveth breath unto the people upon it, and spirit to them that walk therein: I the LORD have called thee in righteousness, and will hold thine hand, and will keep thee, and give thee for a covenant of the people, for a light of the Gentiles.

He is Eternal

Hebrews 9:14: How much more shall the blood of Christ, who through the eternal Spirit offered himself without spot to God, purge your conscience from dead works to serve the living God?

He Teaches

1 Cor. 2:10-13: But God hath revealed them unto us by his Spirit: for the Spirit searcheth all things, yea, the deep things of God. For what man knoweth the things of a man, save the spirit of man which is

in him? even so the things of God knoweth no [one], but the Spirit of God. Now we have received, not the spirit of the world, but the spirit which is of God; that we might know the things that are freely given to us of God. Which things also we speak, not in the words which man's wisdom teacheth, but which the Holy Ghost teacheth; comparing spiritual things with spiritual.

He will Raise the Dead

Romans 8:10-11: But if Christ is in you, although the body is dead because of sin, the Spirit is life because of righteousness. If the Spirit of him who raised Jesus from the dead dwells in you, he who raised Christ Jesus from the dead will also give life to your mortal bodies through his Spirit who dwells in you.

He makes us Children of God

Romans 8:14-16: For all who are led by the Spirit of God are sons of God. For you did not receive the spirit of slavery to fall back into fear, but you have received the Spirit of adoption as sons, by whom we cry, "Abba! Father!" The Spirit himself bears witness with our spirit that we are children of God.

John 3:5: Jesus answered Nicodemus, "Except a man be born of water and the Spirit, he cannot enter into the Kingdom of God.

He is Divine

Isaiah 6:3: And one cried unto another, and said,

"Holy, holy, holy is the LORD of hosts; the whole earth is full of his glory."

His Nature is Truth

John 16:13: Howbeit when he, the Spirit of truth, is come, he will guide you into all truth: for he shall not speak of himself; but whatsoever he shall hear, that shall he speak: and he will show you things to come. He shall glorify me: for he shall receive of mine, and shall show it unto you.

John 17:17: [Jesus, praying for His disciples to be kept from evil] "Sanctify them through thy truth: thy word is truth. As thou sent me into the world, even so I have sent them into the world. And for their sakes I sanctify myself, that they also might be sanctified through the truth."

He is Personal

John 14:26: But the Comforter, which is the Holy Ghost, whom the Father will send in my name, he shall teach you all things, and bring all things to your remembrance, whatsoever I have said unto you.

He Aids Christians in Overcoming Evil

Eph. 6:13-17: Wherefore take unto you the whole armor of God, that ye may be able to withstand in the evil day, and having done all, to stand. Stand therefore, having your loins girt about with truth, and having on the breastplate of righteousness; and your feet shod with the preparation of the gospel of peace. Above all, taking the shield of faith, wherewith ye shall be able to quench all the fiery darts of the wicked. And take the helmet of salvation, and the sword of the Spirit, which is the word of God.

THE PERSONALITY OF THE HOLY SPIRIT

Gary Workman
The Restorer (Vol.7, No. 1, Jan. 1987)

The Holy Spirit has been the most mysterious member of the Godhead. Many, in fact, do not realize that he is a person or being. Perhaps this is partly due to the fact that he does not have what we would consider a personal name. Another reason is that the word "Spirit" in the Greek New Testament is neuter, and therefore the pronoun "it" has appeared in reference to him in some of our English translations (Rom. 8:16—KJV; 1 Pet 1:11— KJV, ASV). A third factor for falling to realize the personality of the Holy Spirit is that there is no recorded statement we can read from him in any biblical conversation.

For these and perhaps other reasons, some have considered him to be impersonal or inanimate in nature. The so-called "Jehovah's Witnesses" refer to him simply as God's active force. But he is much more than some unseen power, some supernatural counterpart to electricity or magnetism or radiation. There is much we cannot know about the Holy Spirit this side of judgment day (Deut. 29:29), but there is also much we can learn. Since the Bible was inspired by the Holy Spirit (2 Pet 1:21; Eph. 6:17), making him its real author (Acts 28:25; Heb. 3:7; 10:15), we ought to learn all we can about him. There are about

90 references to him in the Old Testament and about 263 in the New.

The biblical terms used for the Holy Spirit show that he is a person. The Old Testament gives him a dozen titles and the New Testament nearly forty. Some of these terms could only apply to a being. For example, he is called the "comforter" (John 14:16, 26; 15:26; 16:7), also translated as advocate (as in 1 John 2:1) or helper. As such, he has given "comfort" or encouragement to God's people (Acts 9:31). When the New Testament speaks of him as the Spirit of God or Spirit of Christ (Rom. 8:9; cf. Luke 4:18; Acts 16:6-7), this means much more than the mind, temper, or disposition of God and Christ. For, though the word "Spirit" is neuter in grammatical gender, masculine pronouns are sometimes used of him in the Greek New Testament (John 14:26; 16:13-14), in deference to his actual nature.

The personality of the Holy Spirit is also seen by his characteristics. He has a mind (Rom. 8:27), he has love (Rom. 15:30), and he has fellowship (2 Cor. 13:14; Phil. 2:1). His individuality is further exemplified by his actions. He hears (John 16:13); he searches and knows (1 Cor. 2:10-11); he speaks or declares (Matt 10:20, John 16:13; 1 Tim. 4:1); he teaches and testifies (John 14:26; 15:26); he wills (1 Cor. 14:11); he commands and forbids (Acts 8:29, 16:6-7); and he intercedes in our behalf (Rom. 8:26-27).

Moreover, the Holy Spirit is revealed to be a person by the way men have responded to him. Though the Holy Spirit strives with man through God's revealed will (Gen. 6:3), he has been grieved (Isa. 63:10, Eph. 4:30), lied to (Acts 5:3), resisted (Acts 7:51), blasphemed (Matt 12:31-32) and despitefully mistreated (Heb. 10:29).

The Holy Spirit takes his place, along with the Father and Son, as one of the members of the Godhead (Luke 3:22; Matt 28:19; Rom. 15:30; Eph. 4:4-6, 2 Cor. 13:14). As deity he is said to be omnipotent (Mic. 3:8; Zech. 4:6), omnipresent (Ps. 139:7-10), and eternal (Heb. 9:14). May we ever respect him as "the Spirit of truth" who reveals God's will to us (John 16:13). And may we always appreciate him as "the Spirit of life" (Rom. 8:2) through whom we are born again (John 3:3-5) and thus washed, regenerated, and renewed (Titus 3:5) unto a spiritual relationship that can last forever.

FOUR VIEWS ON THE HOLY SPIRIT

Gary Workman
The Restorer (Vol. 7, No. 1, January 1987)

This issue of *The Restorer* is devoted primarily to a discussion of the Holy Spirit and his relationship to Christians. Of particular interest is the meaning of "the gift of the Holy Spirit" in Acts 2:38 and the nature of the Spirit's indwelling.

Since the beginning of the current movement to restore New Testament. Christianity, brethren have been known to have differing views on some of these questions. It must be admitted by any careful student of the scriptures, no matter what his position, that there are difficulties relating to the subject. If this were not the case, all would be agreed. The fact that varying positions continue to exist among men who are known for their soundness as well as their ability to exegete the scriptures should serve as a caution against radical dogmatism on anyone's part. At least two of the four men engaging in this discussion have changed some of their positions on this subject since the early days of their preaching. And we continue to hear of seasoned preachers re-studying the subject and sometimes altering their views and/or interpretations of certain passages. None of these four writers would countenance an intolerant attitude toward any representative of one of the other views. And all of them would stand as a solid phalanx against any disruption of fellowship over these particular questions, for the controversial aspects do not affect the way we obey our Lord.

The articles that follow are presented in order to encourage further study on these matters. Each of the four writers was invited to contribute an article on the basis of his well-known ability in handling the scriptures, the confidence that brethren have in him, and the fact that his position differs somewhat from the other three. These men are therefore able representatives of their views. Each of them would like to have had more space to develop his arguments and present his explanation of various texts, but space is limited. In some cases we had to make some editorial deletions of less relevant material in order for the articles to be of approximately equal length and, at the same time, fit into this one issue of the paper.

We wish it to be understood that the differences between these articles involve more than the interpretation of just one passage of scripture. One basic difference is whether the Holy Spirit dwells in the Christian personally or just representatively. There are also differences regarding particular passages—whether they speak of the miraculous or the non-miraculous. However, all of these writers agree most emphatically that any miraculous endowments were limited to the first century and phased out of existence as the scriptures themselves predicted (1 Cor.

13:8-13; Eph. 4:8-16). We also want the reader to understand that these articles are not mutually exclusive The writers are far more in agreement on the entire scope of the Holy Spirit and his work than in disagreement. And there is necessarily some overlapping of views even in these areas under discussion. Each writer agrees that Deity dwells in one, in a manner of speaking, through the word (compare John 15:5 with v. 7). However, one view is that the Holy Spirit dwells in us *only* through the word and that "the gift of the Holy Spirit" refers to non-miraculous blessings. Another view differs only in that "the gift of the Holy Spirit" and a few similar expressions are said to refer to the miraculous. A third view accepts a representative indwelling in principle but holds that all specific references to the gift or indwelling of the Holy Spirit are to be understood as miraculous. A fourth view maintains that there is a personal indwelling of the Holy Spirit. We invite your careful attention to each of these articles.

View 1: The Indwelling of the Holy Spirit

Perry B. Cotham
The Restorer (Vol. 7, No. 1, January 1987)

The question of the indwelling of the Spirit in Christians has been one of interest in our brotherhood for a number of years, especially in the last few years due to the rise of the Charismatic Movement. Either the Holy Spirit dwells in the child of God or he does not. If he does indwell, then he either indwells directly or indirectly. Our question at this time is this: "What does the Bible teach regarding the Spirit's indwelling?"

Basic Bible Doctrine

The Bible teaches: (1) that the Holy Spirit is a divine person, one of the eternal members of the Godhead (Matt 28:19, Acts 5:3-4), (2) that the baptism of the Holy Spirit was received by the apostles on Pentecost (Acts 1:4-5, 8; 2:1-4), later by Paul (by implication, 1 Cor. 15:8-9, 2 Cor. 12:12; 1 Cor. 9:1), and by the Gentiles at the house of Cornelius (Acts 10:44-47; 11:15-17), (3) that the miraculous gifts of the Spirit were imparted to some in the early church by the laying on of the apostles' hands (Acts 19:6; 2 Tim. 1:6; 1 Cor. 12:4-11, 28-30), (4) that the baptism in (or with) the Holy Spirit and the miraculous gifts of the Spirit were necessary at the beginning of the church to reveal the truth (1 Cor. 2:7-13), to confirm the word (Mark 16:20; Heb. 2:3-4), and to record the message (Eph. 2:3-5; 2 Tim. 3:16-17), (5) that these miraculous manifestations of the power of the Spirit of God ceased at the completion of this work, being no longer needed, since we now have "the faith once for all delivered unto the saints" (Jude 3, ASV; 1 Cor. 13:8-10, 13; Eph. 4:8, 11-13), (6) that the three persons of the Godhead worked together to bring the scheme of redemption to man, that is, that God the Father planned for man's salvation (Eph. 3:9-11), the Son of God came and executed the plan (Heb. 2:9), and the Holy Spirit revealed, confirmed, and recorded the plan for all future generations establishing the church or Christianity (John 14:26; 16:13), and (7) that Christ had the Spirit without measure (John 3:34; Acts 10:38), implying there are different "measures" or "manifestations" (1 Cor. 2:7) of the Spirit, that is, varying portions of power which the Holy Spirit bestows upon others.

Furthermore, the Bible teaches that in conviction and conversion, and in the sanctification of the child of God, the Holy Spirit exerts his influence on the heart of man only through the revealed word. "The law of the Lord is perfect, converting the soul" (Ps. 19:7; cf. Acts 2:37). One is born again of the Spirit (John 3:5), but man is begotten (born again) by the word (1 Pet 1:23; 1 Cor. 4:15; Jas. 1:18). The spiritual birth is by the Spirit through the medium of the inspired word, the seed of the kingdom (Luke 8:11), and not in some direct, mysterious, miraculous manner over and above and in addition to the word of God. Not only did Paul call "the gospel of Christ" “the power of God unto salvation" (Rom. 1:16), he said that the "sword of the Spirit . . . is the word of God" (Eph. 6:17).

Christians are strengthened by the Spirit through the word as they feed upon the word of God (Eph. 3:16; Acts 20:32). This is how they grow (1 Pet. 2:2). Christians are guided, directed, and led by the Spirit. "For as many as are led by the Spirit of God, they are the sons of God" (Rom. 8:14). But this leading or guidance by the Spirit is through the word. "Thou shalt guide me with thy counsel, and afterward receive me to glory" (Ps. 73:24). "Thy word is a lamp unto my feet, and a light unto my path" (Ps. 119:105). "The entrance of thy words giveth light; it giveth understanding unto the simple" (Ps. 119:130). To the seven churches of Asia John wrote: "He that hath an ear, let him hear what the Spirit saith unto the churches" (Rev. 2:7, 11, 17, 29, 3:6, 13, 22). The Holy Spirit taught the congregations through these letters penned by the inspired apostle. Hence, it is wrong to affirm some kind of direct influence of the Holy Spirit on the heart of man for his salvation, in addition to the word.

How the Spirit indwells

The word of God teaches that in some sense or in some way the Holy Spirit dwells in Christians. Paul said:

> *But ye are not in the flesh, but in the Spirit, if so be that the Spirit of God dwell in you . . . But if the Spirit of him that raised up Jesus from the dead dwell in you, he that raised up Christ from the dead shall also quicken your mortal bodies by his Spirit that dwelleth in you (Rom. 8:9. 11).*

But *how* does the Spirit indwell? There is a difference between stating the *fact* and stating the *method* (the *how*) of the indwelling. The Bible plainly says that the Holy Spirit dwells within Christians, but it does *not* say that the Spirit dwells in them *apart from the inspired word.*

Some think there is no way to determine from the Scriptures how the Spirit indwells the child of God. Others set forth the idea of a direct, personal indwelling separate and apart and in addition to the word of God. To say that the Holy Spirit dwells *directly* in Christians today to give some kind of direct guidance, help, or comfort is to affirm something not taught in the Bible. Yet in the minds of almost all people in the denominational world there is that idea of some kind of personal, direct indwelling of the Spirit in the heart of the child of God, and that the Spirit gives the believer some extra help in addition to the word. This belief leads to all kinds of "experiences" and "feelings." In fact there is no end to this doctrine, if and when it is carried to its logical conclusions.

Now let us carefully note some things:

1. **Christ dwells in Christians.** Paul wrote: ". . . Christ in you, the hope of glory" (Col. 1:27). But *how* does Christ dwell in us? Paul explains: "that Christ may dwell in your hearts through faith" (Eph. 3:17, ASV). Now, how does faith come? Paul answered: "So then faith cometh by hearing, and hearing by the word of God" (Rom. 10:17). So it is not *personally* but through the word of God that Christ dwells in the hearts of Christians (cf. 2 Cor. 13:5).

2. **God dwells in Christians**. The apostle John wrote: "If we love one another, God dwelleth in us" (1 John 4:12; cf. vv. 15-16, 2 Cor. 6:16). But *how* does God indwell his children? Is it direct or indirect? It is indirect, through the word. "And he that keepeth his commandments dwelleth in him, and he in him" (1 John 3:24).

3. **The Holy Spirit dwells in Christians** (1 Cor. 6:19; 3:16). But *how?* The Spirit indwells indirectly, that is, through one's obedience to the word, the same way that God and Christ live in us. They dwell in each faithful member of the church. But neither God, Christ, nor the Holy Spirit dwells *personally* in Christians.

As one obeys the Spirit's message, the Spirit's influences are there in the Christian and he brings forth "the fruit of the Spirit" in his life: "love, joy, peace," etc. (Gal. 5:22, 23). Christians today have the "fruit-bearing measure" of the Holy Spirit, a non-miraculous influence of the Spirit, in their lives. As one has the inspired Spirit's message in his heart when he loves and obeys it, he has in this way the Spirit dwelling in him. This is not the "mere word" or the "dead letter," as some have said. Since there is life in the word (Luke 8:11; John 6:63), the Christian has the living, powerful word of God dwelling in his heart (Heb. 4:12; 1 Pet. 1:25). Thus, the Holy Spirit wields an influence upon us today through the word of God which he gave through the writers of the Bible (cf. Heb. 9:30; Acts 1:16; Eph. 3:3-5; 2 Pet 1:21).

Let us now compare Ephesians 5:17-19 with Colossians 3:16. Both statements are parallel commands from Paul to Christians:

> *Wherefore be ye not unwise, but understanding what the will of the Lord is . . . be filled with the Spirit, speaking to yourselves in psalms and hymns and spiritual songs, singing and making melody in your heart to the Lord (Eph. 5:17-19).*

> *Let the word of Christ dwell in you richly in all wisdom; teaching and admonishing one another in psalms and hymns and spiritual songs, singing with grace in your hearts to the Lord (Col. 3:16).*

For Christians, therefore, to be "filled with the Spirit" is to let "the word of Christ dwell in" them richly. When "the word of Christ" dwells in Christians, the Holy Spirit dwells in them. *There is no statement of Scripture which teaches that the Holy*

Spirit today dwells literally, directly, and personally in the child of God. He indwells the Christian indirectly, that is, through the inspired word of God (2 John 2).

If God the Father and Christ the Son of God can indwell Christians without there being a direct, literal, and personal indwelling—and they do (as is commonly believed)—why cannot the Holy Spirit, the third person of the Godhead, indwell children of God without there being a literal and direct indwelling? The Bible teaches that he does so indwell.

Some, however, believe that the Holy Spirit dwells personally and literally in Christians, but that he does not do anything for them by this direct indwelling—that all leading, guidance, etc. is done only through the word. But why does the Spirit lie dormant in the heart of Christians? Nevertheless, usually many of those who hold to this idea of a direct indwelling will, sooner or later, come to believe that at times the Holy Spirit is actually doing something *to* them in a *direct* way. People often give verses of Scripture that state the *fact* that the Spirit dwells in us, and then *assume* that this means that the Spirit dwells in a direct, literal and personal manner and ignore such statements as Ephesians 3:17 and Colossians 3:16, which explain the *how* of his indwelling.

To quote from the well-known and scholarly Guy N. Woods:

> The fact that the scriptures assert that the

> Spirit dwells in the Christian does not justify the conclusion that this indwelling is personal, immediate, and apart from the word of God (*Commentary on I John.* p. 286).

Likewise, J. W. McGarvey stated it well:

> The fact that the Holy Spirit dwells in us is no proof that his action upon our moral sentiments is direct or immediate (*Original Commentary on Acts*. p. 143).

We agree with the statements of James W. Zachary, a pioneer gospel preacher, when he said:

> The Bible teaches that God dwells in Christians, that Christ lives in Christians, and that the Holy Spirit abides in Christians; but it does *not* teach that either God, Christ, or the Holy Spirit exists in any man in the sense of real personality . . . The personal habitation of God, Christ, and the Holy Spirit is in heaven, and they only dwell in Christians by faith and through the influence of wisely adapted means and medium (*The Witness of the Spirits,* pp. 50-51).

Thus, when the word of God, the Holy Spirit's teaching, is dwelling in the heart of the obedient child of God—leading, guiding, and directing him in living the Christian life—then it can be said that the

Spirit of God is dwelling in him and leading, guiding, and directing his life. The sum of the teaching of the Scriptures on the indwelling of the Holy Spirit is that God, Christ, and the Holy Spirit dwell in Christians today only through one's obedience to the word of truth, that is, metaphorically. The more faithful a child of God is, the more influence of the Holy Spirit he has in his life. That does not mean that it is merely the written word dwelling in him, for that would mean that the person who memorized the most scriptures would have the most of the Holy Spirit. What it means is that as one loves and obeys the word, the Spirit indwells. It is therefore through revelation that Deity indwells us.

The Gift of the Holy Spirit

People often ask, "What did Peter, on Pentecost, mean when he promised 'the gift of the Holy Ghost (Spirit)' to all those who would repent and be baptized for the remission of sins?" Based upon the promise mentioned in Acts 2:38, modern charismatics say that they have the personal, direct indwelling of the Spirit and the baptism of the Holy Spirit. They seem to be unable to make a distinction between the different "measures" or "manifestations" of the Holy Spirit: (1) the baptismal measure, (2) the laying on of hands or miraculous gifts measure, and (3) the ordinary or non-miraculous measure. No one today has the baptism of the Holy Spirit or any of the miraculous gifts of the Spirit, for these measures are no longer needed. All of the truth has been revealed, confirmed, and recorded. The day of miracles has passed. Some think, however, that "the gift of the Holy Spirit" in Acts 2:38 refers to the miraculous gifts of the Spirit which were imparted by the laying on of the apostles' hands and ceased at the close of the apostolic age. But not every baptized believer received miraculous gifts. So they confuse "the gift of the Holy Spirit" with miraculous "gifts" (1 Cor. 12:4).

Moreover, no one now has or has ever had, according to the Bible, a personal, direct indwelling of the Holy Spirit—not even the apostles. The apostles were promised the *power* from the Holy Spirit. Christ said to them before his ascension: ". . . tarry ye in the city of Jerusalem, until ye be endued (clothed, ASV) with power from on high" (Luke 24:49). Later he said: "But ye shall receive power after that the Holy Ghost is come upon you" (Acts 1:8), and ". . . ye shall be baptized with (in, ASV) the Holy Ghost not many days hence" (Acts 1:5). This POWER of the Spirit, a divine person, was necessary for the revelation, inspiration, confirmation, and spreading of the gospel to all the world. But not one word of evidence can be found that the Spirit came into them and dwelt directly or literally inside their bodies.

The apostles had the *power*—the effects—of the Holy Spirit. This is a figure of speech known as *metonymy*—the cause for the effect. For example, in Luke 11:13 the "Holy Spirit" refers to the "good things" of the Spirit as mentioned in Matthew 7:11.

The cause is named, but the effect is meant. The Holy Spirit himself is not measured out but the *portion of power* he gives is. The words "baptism," "enduement," and "filling" all refer to one and the same experience. So the apostles on Pentecost "were all filled with the Holy Ghost" (Acts 2:4)—that is, they had the miraculous power from the Holy Spirit to do their work. This was the baptism of the Spirit

Later, Peter and John went down to the city of Samaria, after Philip had preached there, so that the recently baptized believers might "receive the Holy Ghost" (Acts 8:14-18)—that is, that they might impart unto them the miraculous gifts of the Spirit which only the apostles could bestow (Acts 6:6, 8) and which were necessary in that early day of the church in the absence of the written New Testament scriptures. So these Samaritans received the Spirit, they received the miraculous powers of the Spirit which Philip could not impart. (Here again is metonymy.) But they did not receive a direct personal indwelling of the Holy Spirit

In Acts 2:38, did Peter mean that the ones baptized would receive the Holy Spirit himself in person as a gift, or receive that which the Holy Spirit had to give? These words must be understood in the full teaching of the Bible on the subject. We should compare "the gift of the holy Spirit" with the phrases "the gift of God" (John 4:10, Rom. 6:23) and "the gift of Christ" (Eph. 4:7); they mean a gift *from* God and a gift *from* Christ, not. God and Christ as a gift. If one should be told to do something in order to "receive the gift of John Doe (a person)," what would that naturally imply?

If we compare Acts 2:38 with Acts 3:19, given later by Peter, it will help us to understand "the gift of the Holy Spirit." The two verses are parallel; they mean exactly the same thing.

Acts 2:38	Acts 3:19
1. Repent	1. Repent
2. Be baptized	2. Be converted (turn again)
3. Remission of sins	3. Sins blotted out
4. Gift of the Holy Spirit	4. Times of refreshing from the Lord

Therefore, receiving the blessings or "refreshing" from the Lord (a figurative expression) is the same as receiving "the gift of the Holy Spirit." Both statements refer to receiving the spiritual blessings that follow after one is baptized into Christ

Let us now compare these two verses with Paul's language in 1 Corinthians 12:13;

> *For by one Spirit are we all baptized into one body, whether we be Jews or Gentiles, whether we be bond or free; and have been all made to drink into one Spirit*

This means that by the teaching of the Holy Spirit (through the word) we are baptized (immersed in water, Rom. 6:3-4) into the one body, the church (Eph.

1:22-23), and are privileged "to drink into one Spirit," that is, to enjoy the blessings provided by the Spirit in Christ. Jesus (cf. 2 Cor. 5:17; Gal. 4:6, Eph. 1:3). The church is a spiritual kingdom, entered by a spiritual birth, and in it are spiritual blessings.

Receiving "the gift of the Holy Spirit" in Acts 2:38 therefore means receiving the Holy Spirit—receiving the blessings from the Spirit. Here again is the use of the figure of speech known as metonymy—that which the Holy Spirit gives. All baptized believers today receive the remission of their sins and enter into Christ where are all spiritual blessings, but they do not receive any of the miraculous gifts of the Spirit or any kind of direct, literal, personal indwelling of the Spirit, whether to be inactive in them or to illuminate, guide, strengthen, and give them joy in living the Christian life. If the Holy Spirit dwelt directly in a Christian, that would be miraculous. All the influence of the Holy Spirit on the heart of man for his salvation is only through the inspired word.

So, the "measure" of "the gift of the Holy Spirit" in Acts 2:38 must not be equated with either the baptism of the Spirit or the receiving of any of the miraculous gifts of the Spirit or a personal, direct indwelling of the Spirit. Nevertheless, the three "measures" or "manifestations" of the Holy Spirit spoken of in the New Testament are each called the "gift" of the Spirit—namely, (1) the baptism of the Spirit (Acts 1:5; 10:44-45; 11:15-17), (2) the miraculous gifts of the Spirit (Rom. 1:11; 1 Cor. 12:1, 4-

11; 2 Tim. 1:6), and (3) the common or ordinary (non-miraculous) gift of the Spirit (Acts 2:38). But all of these "measures" do not imply the same portion of power from the Holy Spirit. The word "gift" does not tell what “manifestation" of the Spirit is under consideration. The context must determine which "gift" is meant. But not every statement in the New Testament that mentions the Holy Spirit refers to the miraculous. A person might give to one man a gift of one dollar and that would be as much a gift as if he would give to another man a gift of five dollars, and to another one a gift of ten dollars.

David Lipscomb, commenting on Acts 2:38 and the presence of the Holy Spirit in all Christians, made this clear statement:

> By receiving and cherishing the word in the heart, the Spirit enters and abounds more and more in the person, making him like Jesus in his thoughts, feelings, works. I feel sure this is the manifestation of the Spirit promised to those who would repent and be baptized . . . This Spirit enters the heart with and through the word of God, and spreads and strengthens as the word of God, the seed of the kingdom, more and more is understood and cherished in the heart (*Queries and Answers.* pp. 206. 207).

Conclusion

Our conclusion is that the Bible teaches that men

have had the Holy Spirit in different measures, or varying portions of power, but that all power of the Holy Spirit today in the hearts of men is only through the word of God. In this manner the Spirit indwells the Christian the same way in which God and Christ indwell. As children of God cherish the Spirit's message in their hearts and live by it in their lives, the Holy Spirit dwells in them, and collectively in the church. Everyone who becomes obedient receives the benefits provided by the Spirit in this Christian dispensation. "All scripture is given by inspiration of God . . . that the man of God may be perfect, throughly furnished unto all good works" (2 Tim. 3:16, 17).

VIEW 2: WHAT IS THE GIFT OF THE HOLY SPIRIT IN ACTS 2:38?

Robert R. Taylor, Jr.
The Restorer (Vol. 7, No. 1, January 1987)

There is an abounding interest in the answer to this question. For well over thirty-five years I have been a student of this passage in general and this part of it in particular. I have tried to read widely relative to what our brethren have written on this passage. I have often asked brethren what they thought it meant. Brethren, with frequency, have asked my thoughts about its meaning. It seems to me that there have been three main positions our brethren have sustained toward it.

1. Many, perhaps most of our brotherhood, espouse the position that this refers to the common, ordinary gift of the Holy Spirit's indwelling the Christian and comes at the very same time that remission of sins or pardon is tendered to the obeying individual. It would be their contention that every person who has been saved from Pentecost in Acts 2 to the present has been a sure recipient of this common, ordinary gift. Many of this number would say the Holy Spirit comes into the individual actually, personally, bodily and literally, though some would say he indwells the Christian through a medium—the word of

God—and hence the indwelling is representative.

2. Others contend that the gift of the Holy Spirit is the equivalent of pardon—that this gift is what the Holy Spirit gives (and is not himself a gift), with that gift as pardon of past sins. Some would extend it a bit and say the gift is the equivalent of eternal life in yonder's world. Since Peter had already promised fullness of pardon in the expression—"remission of sins"—it seems a bit redundant that Peter would repeat himself with another expression that means only what he had already promised them. To make the gift the equivalent of eternal life is to ignore the remainder of the Bible which teaches that Christian faithfulness is the condition of going home to heaven for the penitent believer who has been immersed.

3. The third contention, one I have long held and defended, is that the tendered gift here is miraculous in that context and would be conferred upon them, as explained by subsequent scriptures, by apostolic imposition of hands. Obviously, it could not be possessed by anyone save those to whom the apostles transmitted it by the laying on of their hands. This is the position I shall seek to explain and defend in the remnant of this study.

An Analysis of the Passage

Acts 2:38 in fullness states.

> *Then Peter said unto them, Repent, and be baptized every one of you in the name of Jesus Christ for the remission of sins, and*

> *ye shall receive the gift of the Holy Ghost (Spirit—ASV).*

Peter has the keys to the kingdom (Matt 16:18). He and his apostolic colleagues have been asked the most crucial question of the ages in the preceding verse—what to do to be saved. Peter calls upon them as convicted believers in Christ to repent. Repentance is a change of mind. Godly sorrow precedes it, amended life is its forthcoming fruit. His second stipulation is baptism. This is immersion; water is the element. The commands are addressed to every one of them. Their obedience was to be done in the name of Jesus (Savior) Christ (the anointed One). This means by his authority. He who possessed all authority in heaven and on earth commanded baptism (Matt. 28:18-19). "For" means in order to obtain this coveted pardon. Remission of sins is forgiveness, pardon, becoming saved, having sins washed away, or having sins blotted out (cf. Mark 16:16; Acts 22:16; 3:19).

"And ye shall receive the gift of the Holy Ghost" *And* means something in addition to pardon—not pardon alone or exclusively. *Ye* is a personal pronoun. It is the subject of this expression. *Shall receive* is the predicate or the verb. It is a transitive verb and as such requires a direct object. The object here has to be in the accusative case. Obviously, Spirit is not that object. *Spirit,* as used in this expression, is in the possessive case as we view it from the English language. It is the Spirit's gift, or that which he confers. The direct object is the word *gift,* which is in the accusative case. *Gift* here is not the Holy Spirit. To the woman at Jacob's well Jesus spoke of "the gift of God" (John 4:10). This is not God but something God gives. In eloquent Ephesians Paul speaks of "the gift of Christ" (Eph. 4:7). This was not the gift of Christ himself but something Christ gave. The same is true with the gift of the Holy Spirit it was not the Holy Spirit given but something the Spirit gave.

This is a short and accurate analysis of the verse in general and of the controversial part. I am examining *the gift of the Holy Spirit* in particular.

Why Take the Miraculous Measure Position?

For twenty or more years now it has been my sustained position that the gift of the Holy Spirit in Acts 2:38 is the miraculous measure of the Holy Spirit and was transmitted by apostolic imposition of hands on that and subsequent occasions. From a comprehensive study of such passages as Acts 8 and 19 and Romans 1:11 we learn that this miraculous transmitting could not occur without the presence of one or more of the apostles. Such poses no problem in Acts 2, for all twelve of the apostles were present with the ability to transmit such supernatural powers. Some might object by saying that my position is in jeopardy due to the fact that other scriptures are necessary to deduce such a conclusion. But this no more negates my position than other positions taken relative to the gift of Acts 2:38, for they also require additional information derived from kindred passages. The objection might have some merit if there were nothing else said on the matter. However, more is said, and logical reasoning demands a comprehensive contemplation of ALL that is said. But why take this miraculous measure position on Acts 2:38? Let us note several weighty reasons for this view.

1. Acts 2:38 was first given in the first century—not the twentieth century—and in a supernatural framework at that! In Acts 2 we have Holy Spirit baptism upon the twelve (vv. 1-4). In Acts 2 we have supernatural tongue speaking (v. 4ff). In Acts 2 we have an inspired message given by all the apostles at first and by Peter individually from verse 14 onward. Acts 2 is NOT set within an ordinary situation at all, but in a most extraordinary setting. Yet, we are often assured that when Peter promised the gift of the Holy Spirit he was speaking about a totally non-miraculous or ordinary gift. Such is amazing. Objectors to my view have frequently countered my arguments by stating or asking. "What is the natural, normal conclusion WE should reach in surveying the statement 'ye shall receive the gift of the Holy Spirit'?" Much more apropos is how its *initial auditors* understood it, being as they were in the very midst of miraculous might, of supernatural signs, and not of just an ordinary occasion of non-miraculous activity. Instead of trying to place that Pentecost audience in a twentieth-

century setting when that verse was first uttered, would it not be a thousand times more profitable to place ourselves in that first-century setting to understand the gift of the Holy Spirit as they understood it initially? Yes, verily!

2. The Greek term for "gift" here is of wonderful weight in this momentous matter. It derives from *dorea*. In Acts 8:20 Peter employs this term in speaking of the very gift erring Simon sought to purchase with silver from Peter and John. Surely, none among us will take the position that the gift in Acts 8:20 refers to that which was ordinary or non-miraculous! This word is used in Acts 10:45 to describe what came on Cornelius and his household, and Peter used the same expression in Acts 11:17 in his defense against objecting Jewish brethren at Jerusalem. Surely, this was not the ordinary or the non-miraculous. Paul used this term in Ephesians 3:7 and 4:7. Both verses are set in a context where the miraculous is being discussed. This same term is employed in Acts 2:38. It would be strange indeed if *dorea*, or one of its derivatives, in all these other parallel allusions is supernatural or miraculous in meaning and yet is NON-MIRACULOUS and ORDINARY in Acts 2:38.

3. Additional sustaining proof is ascertained from the fact that the expression "gift of the Holy Spirit" occurs but twice in the Bible. One of these is in Acts 2:38; the other is in Acts 10:45 at Cornelius' house-

hold. I know of no one in our brotherhood who dis-associates Acts 10:45 from miraculous activity. It was the baptismal measure in Acts 10:45 which constituted it as the miraculous; it was the laying-on-of-the-apostolic-hands measure in Acts 2:38. In Acts 2 and 10 Luke described what came on Jews and Gentiles respectively at the beginning of the gospel for both races. There is the miraculous on both occasions. Yet, and this is amazingly amazing, in the use of this strikingly similar statement we are told again and again that the Acts 2:38 reference is definitely the non-miraculous or ordinary but that the Acts 10:45 reference is definitely miraculous and not the ordinary at all. That which came in Acts 10:45 came directly from heaven; that which was promised so preciously in Acts 2:38 came by apostolic imposition of hands which had been received directly from heaven for the transmitting of such. Truly, both occasions demand the supernatural—not one the ordinary and the other the extraordinary.

4. The wonderful weight of the word "receive" is clear, cogent and convincing in this momentous matter. "Receive" is employed by Peter in Acts 2:38. Yet, "receive" is used with stirring frequency in sacred scriptures (both KJV and ASV) where supernatural signs involving the Holy Spirit are evident. Jesus employed "receive" in John 7:39 and the miraculous is there VERY evident. "Receive" is used in John 20:23—"Receive ye the Holy Ghost (Spirit—ASV)." Though some would deny the miraculous

link to John 7:39. I know of none who would do it with John 20:23. "Receive" is employed in Acts 8:15-17 with the apostolic transmission of miraculous power to the recently immersed Samaritans by Peter and John. Paul inquired of a dozen Ephesians in Acts 19 if they had "received" the Holy Spirit since they believed (or since they were saved). Paul was surely thinking of the miraculous when he raised the query. "Receive" is again employed among the Galatians in their reception of the miraculous (Gal. 3:1ff). Peter, in Acts 10:47, referred to the miraculous reception of the Holy Spirit as proof positive that Gentiles were worthy of kingdom entrance and should not be denied immersion in water. The anointing in 1 John 2:27 is doubtless miraculous in nature. John used the word "received" in this apostolic allusion to the same. To deny that John here is speaking of the miraculous would be strange indeed. Since "receive" is the very word employed both by the KJV and ASV translators—148 strong—to convey instance after instance of where the miraculous was received, it seems mighty conclusive that such is its stately significance in Acts 2:38 also.

5. The fundamental fact that apostles were present and could transmit this power to the now-to-be-baptized disciples is strong and convincing. People were there by the masses and from all over the known world. Soon, very soon, they would return home again. Each one could not take an apostle home with

him; each one could not take a written New Testament home with him since not the first word of such had yet been composed. They would return to home-country people who would need to see visible evidence miraculously demonstrated to prove they spoke for God. The twelve could transmit such. Are we to understand that they sent them *all* home with neither a written new covenant nor any audible, visual, demonstrative way of proving conclusively the validity of each proclaimed message? Did they go home unaided by ANY transmitted power and just say, "We have the ordinary gift of the Holy Spirit as proof positive that we speak for the now-crowned King of kings and Lord of lords"? Did the apostles deliberately leave them in this highly unarmed condition as they left Jerusalem? If this happened, how strange as per the apostles' subsequent interest in conferring such powers on the Samaritans, Paul's desire to do the same for the dozen Ephesian men in Acts 19, and Paul's driving desire to do so to the Romans in Romans 1:11. Are we then to conclude that the apostles in Acts 2 felt NO need to endow or equip with miraculous powers the initial converts to the Beginning Cause? Let no one say that they did confer such but just did not mention it. That would be a mere conjecture or assumption, and it files in the very face of the fact that the apostles did confer such and told them beforehand of what was to come by referring to "the gift of the Holy Spirit"

6. The miraculous measure of the Holy Spirit in

Acts 2:38 is reasonable. In fact, it is my long-held conviction that it is a far more reasonable position than is the commonly held view of the ordinary gift. Apostolic power was there to confer it, and people were there to receive it who needed it so desperately before they departed Jerusalem for the four corners of the then-inhabited earth with a brand new religion to impart to the world of the lost. Did the apostles totally ignore this obvious need and send them home ill-equipped to spread the good news of redemption and back it up with supernatural confirmation? I, for one, cannot believe they did.

7. In my judgment this is an eminently scriptural view. It makes for full and fervent harmony between Acts 2:38 and Mark 16:16-18. In Mark 16:16 the baptized believer is promised salvation. Then miraculous signs would follow. They are specified in verses 17 and 18. Apostles obviously performed such by the Holy Spirit baptismal measure. Apostolic converts in those initial days of early Christianity performed the miraculous by having apostolic hands laid on them. In Acts 2:38 penitent, baptized believers are promised pardon. Then, quite naturally and in the context of full miraculous activities, they are promised the miraculous gift of the Holy Spirit, enabling them to perform what was promised in Mark 16:17-18. I do not have a particle of a problem understanding Mark 16:17-18 even though it is immediately subsequent to Mark 16:16 and the promise to pardon each baptized believer. Neither do I have a

particle of a problem with the miraculous gift measure of the Holy Spirit in Acts 2:38 even though it comes on the very heels of the promise to pardon each baptized penitent. Acts 2:38 and 3:19 also are marvelous in their precious parallels. Both demand repentance. The baptism of Acts 2:38 obviously equates with "be converted" or "turn again" of Acts 3:19 in the KJV and ASV respectively. Acts 2:38 promises remission of sins; Acts 3:19 promises the blotting out of sins. Acts 2:38 promises the gift of the Holy Spirit. Acts 3:19 promises seasons of refreshing from the presence of the Lord. Many who contend that Acts 2:38 refers to the ordinary gift of the Spirit (same as seasons of refreshing as per their view) will immediately argue that the Spirit confers no blessing upon them other than the natural or ordinary. Yet, as brother Guy H. Woods has stated so sagely, the personal indwelling of the spirit as per their theory,

> (a) gives them no awareness of his presence, (b) teaches them no truth, (c) and requires them to resort to a Book nineteen hundred years old to learn his will through study when he is actually there and in direct contact with the heart (understanding) all the time! Is it any cause for wonder that those who dwell upon an alleged actual personal indwelling of the Spirit go on, like Pat Boone, to believe that the Spirit does indeed move them to act apart from, and independent of the word of truth—the New

> Testament (Guy N. Woods. *Questions and Answers.* Open forum. Freed-Hardeman College Lectures, Nashville. Williams, 1976, pp. 56, 57).

Five Consequences of Other Positions

1. To contend for just the ordinary gift measure here in this sacred text is to deprive the apostles from using the special power of imparting miraculous gifts by imposition of apostolic hands.

2. Furthermore, it would mean that they sent the newly baptized disciples to the four winds with neither a completed Bible in their hands nor any transmitted power to confirm supernaturally what they uttered by word of mouth. Can it so be? I do not believe so.

3. If the Spirit indwells us bodily, personally, actually and directly, then how would Christians avoid being Deity, at least partially? The incarnation of our blessed Saviour was Deity in human flesh as he came to pitch his tent among the masses of men. It makes no appreciable difference whether the Deity that so indwells is that of the Second Person or that of the Third Person of the Godhead.

4. To make the gift of the Holy Spirit a synonym for salvation is to make Peter guilty of redundancy in word usage. Salvation had already been encompassed in the eloquent expression "remission of sins." Acts 2:39 has a strong theological link with Genesis 12:3 which makes crystal clear that salvation

is for Jews, Jewish children (accountable beings, obviously), and for those afar off (Gentiles).

5. To make the gift the exact equivalent of eternal life, and upon terms of repentance and baptism which were necessary for pardon of past sins, is a failure to realize that the condition of going home to heaven, subsequent to entering the Saving Christ, is a faithful life (Matt 25:21, 23). Peter makes this crystal clear in giving the Christian graces in 2 Peter 1:5-11. One must cultivate these soul virtues to enter abundantly the heavenly kingdom on high at last

No Strength Hereby Offered to Current Charismatics

Be it recalled that spiritual gifts (all nine of them—1 Cor. 12:8-10) could *only* be transmitted by Holy Spirit baptism or by apostolic imposition of hands. There have been no Holy Spirit baptisms since Acts 10. That is why Paul could affirm twenty-one years later that there is only one baptism, i.e., Great Commission immersion in water. This is the one and only baptism for us (Eph. 4:5). Hence, we have no recipients of Holy Spirit baptism today. Their only other way of reception was by imposition of apostolic hands. No such is still available! Hence, we have no miraculous measures of the Spirit at work or in evidence in our era. My position on Acts 2:38 will allow for no such miraculous gifts today—not even one! Those who claim possession of such today should be pressed relentlessly to demonstrate it.

This is Not a New or Novel View

A dozen years ago I defended this view in a California lectureship. A veteran preacher present took issue and said he had *never* heard such before. 1 was amazed in that I had been acquainted with the view since I was just a young preacher. Brother Franklin Camp's book on the Holy Spirit, to which I wrote the Foreword, was already out at that time and now has been out for nearly thirteen years. Brother Camp takes this same view as I have just expressed. On pages 131, 132 of the Camp classic, *The Work of the Holy Spirit,* he quotes from David Lipscomb, T.W. Brents, H. Leo Boles, and Alexander Campbell who all said it may or did refer to miraculous powers to be conferred by apostolic imposition of hands. All these men quoted by brother Camp have been dead for decades. Campbell has been dead over 120 years. Brother Guy N. Woods has held this view for more than forty years. Joe Warlick, likely the greatest debater of modern times, held this view. Alan E. Highers holds this view. So do many other eminent Bible scholars among us. I have not quoted these to prove the doctrine is true, but only to show that the view is neither new nor novel. The doctrine must be decided as true or false on the basis of whether the Bible teaches it or falls to so teach. Anyone remotely acquainted with the works of Campbell, Lipscomb, Brents, Boles, Woods, Warlick, Camp, and Highers would *never* accuse these men of advocating modern charismatic gifts for either the nineteenth or twentieth centuries! I think no one acquainted with my preaching, writing, and lecturing across the years will so accuse me either!

Conclusion

I want to go on record again, as I have so many times in the past, that I do not reject an indwelling of Father, Son and Holy Spirit in Christians today. I so believe; I so teach; I so defend! I do not believe it is personal, actual, bodily, literal, direct etc. Deity surely indwells us without question or quibble. The Father indwells us (1 John 4:15). Christ is in us (Col. 1:27). The Holy Spirit is in us (Rom. 8:9). But they do NOT indwell us actually, literally, bodily, personally and directly, in my seasoned judgment. As Deity's will is in us, moves us, and molds us, to that extent God the Father, God the Son, and God the Holy Spirit indwell us. Ephesians 3:17 is a key passage in understanding this momentous matter of wonderful weight. Paul wrote, ". . . that Christ may dwell in your hearts by faith; that ye being rooted and grounded in love . . ." Colossians 3:16 urges us to allow the word of Christ to dwell in us richly. On what other rational ground could one person indwell another person than in this way?

Many who knew my late father, a wonderful Christian for more than fifty years before he died in 1971, and have known me as well, have often remarked how they see my Dad in me. Yet he has never been in me actually, personally, bodily, literally, directly, etc.—not even when he was alive and we lived in the same house as I grew up. He has been and is yet in me to the extent, and this extent ONLY, as his teaching, example, ideals, etc., have and do move and mold me.

VIEW 3: THE GIFT OF THE HOLY SPIRIT

Bobby Duncan
The Restorer (Vol. 7, No. 1, January 1987)

I was somewhat reluctant to accept the invitation to write this article, in view of the disposition of some to brand as unsound and unworthy of fellowship any who differ with them on any subject. As I understand it, the articles in this issue of *The Restorer* all represent differing views of the subject of the indwelling of the Holy Spirit. Until these articles are published I will not have read what all the other writers have said, but I am under the impression that none writing articles for this paper will advance any view which is in conflict with the idea that the only way the Spirit communicates with anyone today is through that which is written in the Bible. In other words, we are all in complete agreement on this point. So long as this is true, I want it to be understood that I do not consider those who differ with the view I will present as holding to "dangerous" views with reference to the matter. During the more than twenty years I have held the view I now hold I have never made the matter a test of fellowship nor have I had any reservations about recommending preachers for jobs and for meetings simply because they differed with me on this matter.

I am confident that the view I will present will not differ greatly from one of the views presented elsewhere in this issue. It is my understanding that another writer will present the view that the "gift of the Holy Ghost" of Acts 2:38 is a reference to the miraculous gifts which were imparted through the laying on of the hands of the apostles. I firmly believe this view to be correct. Acts 8 and Acts 19 are clear examples of this. The difference is in our interpretation of certain other passages that mention the indwelling of the Holy Ghost.

Receiving the Holy Ghost

To say that the "gift of the Holy Ghost" is not the Holy Ghost himself, but that which the Holy Ghost gives is correct. But there is a sense in which that which the Holy Ghost gives is referred to as the Holy Ghost himself. Acts 8:15 says the apostles came from Jerusalem that the people of Samaria might "receive the Holy Ghost." The context shows it was speaking figuratively of the miraculous powers of the Holy Ghost which would be imparted. Verse 17 says they "received the Holy Ghost" and verse 18 says, "the Holy Ghost was given." Did they not *"receive* the *gift* of the Holy Ghost" the very thing Peter mentions in Acts 2:38?

In Acts 19:2 Paul asked: "Have ye received the Holy Ghost since ye believed?" Then verse 6 tells us that "When Paul had laid his hands upon them, the

Holy Ghost came on them; and they spake with tongues, and prophesied." What they actually and literally received was power supplied by the Holy Ghost.

Acts 10:47 says that the household of Cornelius "received the Holy Ghost." Verse 45 says it was "the gift of the Holy Ghost" which they received. They did not literally receive the Holy Ghost as a person, but by a figure of speech which we call *metonymy of the cause,* it is said that they received the Holy Ghost when, in fact, they received power given to them by the Holy Ghost. In explaining this occasion to the other apostles and brethren at Jerusalem, Peter said, "And as I began to speak, the Holy Ghost fell on them, as on us at the beginning" (Acts 10:15).

In all of these cases it is undeniably true that those who received the Holy Ghost received some miraculous manifestation of the power of the Holy Ghost. I am not suggesting that all of these received the same power, or that the Holy Ghost came upon all of them for the same purpose; such simply is not the case. But these passages, which are so plain, teach us what it meant in New Testament times for people to receive the Holy Ghost. One of the elementary rules of Bible study which we all recognize is that we are to allow plain passages to interpret those that are obscure. When I read some passage in the New Testament which mentions someone's receiving or possessing the Holy Ghost and the immediate context of the passage does not make it clear what is meant, I can depend on these passages which do tell what it means to receive the Holy Ghost. This is the kind of logic we use in reasoning with our friends about the action of baptism. If we did not know the meaning of the Greek word translated "baptize," we could learn what it means from Romans 6:4 and Colossians 2:12. Having learned the meaning of the word from these two passages, we would know exactly what the word means when we find it in other passages in the New Testament. Why is that sound reasoning with reference to baptism, but not with reference to the Holy Ghost?

One might say that there are other passages which make it clear that references to receiving or possessing the Holy Ghost were to a non-miraculous indwelling. Let me make it clear that I firmly believe the father, the Son, and the Holy Ghost dwell in Christians. 1 John 4:15 clearly shows that the father dwells in us; Colossians 1:27 shows just as clearly that the Son dwells in us. All of us understand this to mean they dwell in us as we are influenced and developed by their written will. In this same sense, and only in this sense, the Holy Ghost dwells in us. *But. I doubt there is a single verse in the New Testament which refers to one's having the Spirit (Holy Ghost) that is not talking about possessing the Spirit in some miraculous way.*

Please keep in mind that not a single line of the New Testament was written to people like us. Those who lived in a time when miracles had ceased and who had a copy of the New Testament to guide and direct them. Instead they lived in an age of miracles, when they were dependent upon the miraculous gifts of the Holy Ghost to furnish for them what the written New Testament would furnish for those who would live after the revelation of God's will was completed. This faithful brethren have affirmed for years. If you had lived in that time and had received some miraculous power through the laying on of the hands of an apostle, and if that apostle wrote a letter to you and made mention of the fact that you had received the Spirit, what would you think he was talking about? Would you think he was referring to some non-miraculous, personal indwelling of the Spirit? No. You would understand this reference to be to that which you had received through the laying on of the hands of the apostle.

For example, the church at. Corinth had an abundance of miraculous gifts (1 Cor. 1:7; 2 Cor. 12:12, 13). When Paul told them their body was the temple of the Holy Ghost (1 Cor. 6:19), what do you supposed came to their minds? When he said, "I have the Spirit of God" (7:40), what did they think he meant? When he said the Spirit of God dwelt in them (3:16), what would they understand him to be saying? Let us not forget that the proper understanding of any passage is the precise idea which the Holy Ghost intended to convey to those people to whom the passage was originally written. Therefore, we make a great mistake if we try to interpret passages which have to do with the miraculous as if they were originally written to people like us, who live in a non-miraculous age and have a written New Testament. We have no trouble recognizing this principle in dealing with such passages as John 14:26, John 16:13 and Mark 16:17.

Various Passages Considered

It is sometimes argued that it was said of John the Baptist that he would be "filled with the Holy Ghost" (Luke 1:15), and yet. John 10:41 says that John did no miracle. Therefore, John must have been filled with the Holy Ghost in a non-miraculous way. But this line of reasoning misses the point of either one or both of the passages cited. John 10:41 is talking about the fact that John did not perform miracles—like Jesus or the apostles performed—to confirm the word he preached. But who would say that John was not an inspired preacher? This is what is meant by the statement in Luke 1:15, which says he would be "filled with the Holy Ghost." Two other times in that same chapter it is said that certain ones were "filled with the Holy Ghost," and both times those so filled uttered inspired speeches. Verse 41 says Elizabeth was filled with the Holy Ghost and verse 67 says Zacharias was filled with the Holy Ghost. It was in this same sense that John was to be filled with the Holy Ghost—not in some non-miraculous sense, or merely as he would be influenced by the written word of God. Matthew 21:23-27 bears out this fact. The baptism which John administered was from

God, but it was not something John was taught to do by the written word of God. Obviously he did it by direct revelation and inspiration.

Paul told the Ephesians that they were sealed with the Holy Spirit (Eph. 1:13). In the next verse he told them that the Holy Spirit was the earnest of their inheritance. The very idea of a seal or that which serves as an earnest demands something tangible. They were scaled, or received this earnest, when Paul laid his hands on them, and they spoke with tongues and prophesied (Acts 19:5).

To the Galatians Paul wrote: "This only would I learn of you, Received ye the Spirit by the works of the law, or by the hearing of faith?" (Gal. 3:2). The Galatians were being disturbed by Judaizing teachers, those trying to bind upon them the keeping of the law of Moses. If Paul could get them to see that God approved of their obedience to the gospel separate and apart from the law of Moses, then the Judaizing teachers would be defeated. To do this, Paul simply asks in what connection they received the Spirit. Was it in connection with the keeping of the law, or was it in connection with their obedience to the gospel? If Paul is talking about a miraculous reception of the Spirit, then his question would be quite easy for them to answer. They knew those Judaizing teachers had not imparted to them any miraculous powers. They knew also that they had received miraculous powers of the Spirit by the laying on of the hands of an apostle, after they had obeyed the gospel of Christ. Verse

5 shows this is exactly what is under consideration: “He therefore that ministereth to you the Spirit and worketh miracles among you, doeth he it by the works of the law, or by the hearing of faith?"

Romans 8:9 is sometimes used to show that all who belong to Christ must have the Holy Spirit dwelling in them: "Now if any man have not the Spirit of Christ he is none of his.” I will admit that this chapter is a very difficult one, and not merely to one who may hold the position I do with reference to the indwelling of the Holy Ghost. But before I comment on the verse before us, I would urge the reader to remember that the work of the Holy Ghost in connection with the scheme of redemption has always been to reveal the mind of God to man and to confirm that revelation by the performing of miracles. One in the first century who preached the word of God proved that what he had was the word of God by the miraculous manifestations of the Holy Spirit. In other words, preachers in apostolic days used the Holy Spirit to prove that they had the word of God, preachers in our day use the word of God to try to prove they have the Holy Spirit. What in the context of Romans 8:9 would lead Paul to make a statement to the effect that all who belong to Christ have the Spirit dwelling in them in a non-miraculous way? On the other hand, Judaism was the problem being dealt with in the book of Romans. But the Judaizing teachers could not confirm their false teaching by the performing of miracles. Those who preached the gospel could so confirm what they preached. Paul is reminding them of this fact in the latter part of this particular verse. If a man came teaching a doctrine which could not be confirmed by the performing of miracles, then he was to be considered a false teacher. Incidentally, Thayer's Lexicon (p. 612) says that the expression "In the Spirit" in the first part of this very verse means "to be in the power of, be actuated by, inspired by, the Holy Spirit. I personally do not believe Paul switched in the middle of the verse from the miraculous to the non-miraculous indwelling of the Spirit

Two Prominent Passages

What about the promise of Acts 2:39? The book of Luke closes with an account of Christ's ascension. Before he ascended, he said, "And, behold, I send the promise of my Father upon you. . ." (Luke 24:49). This is an obvious reference to the miraculous outpouring of the Holy Ghost. As Luke takes up the narrative in Acts 1, he refers to the Lord's admonition to "wait for the promise of the Father" (Acts 1:4)—another reference to supernatural power. After the outpouring of the Holy Ghost in Acts 2. Peter explained that what they had seen and heard was in connection with "the promise of the Holy Ghost" (2:33). Then after telling the people what to do to receive remission of sins, he said, "For the promise is unto you..." (v. 39). Now, suppose you are Theophilus, and Luke had written the books of Luke and Acts to you. Would you get the impression that Peter was promising some non-miraculous gift of the Holy Ghost to those people? Or if you had been one of those Jews present on Pentecost and had seen and heard what they had seen and heard, would you think Peter was talking about a non-miraculous indwelling of the Spirit? I say again that what the apostles received and what others received upon whom the apostles laid their hands was not identical. The Holy Ghost came upon them for different purposes and to impart different powers. But the receiving of the Holy Ghost was the reception of miraculous powers of the Holy Ghost.

Some say that the language of Acts 2:39 demands that the gift of the Holy Ghost is promised to all in every age who would repent and be baptized, and therefore could not refer to those miraculous gifts which were limited to the apostolic age. "For the promise is unto you, and to your children, and to all that are afar off, even as many as the Lord our God shall call." But remember that Peter had quoted earlier in this speech a prophecy which said that the Spirit would be poured out upon "all flesh." Does "all flesh" mean literally all flesh? If you can explain that it means simply that Jews and Gentiles alike would have the Spirit poured out on them, then you should have little difficulty in understanding how "all that are afar off" might not mean literally all that are afar off. You may not agree, but at least you can see the point.

Some assert that Acts 5:32 proves that all Christians have the Holy Spirit dwelling in them: "And we are witnesses of these things: and so is also the Holy Ghost, whom God hath given to them that obey him" (Acts 5:32). Before discussing this verse, I would remind the reader again that those in the first century who had the Holy Ghost used it to prove that they had the word of God; they never had to use the word of God to prove they had the Holy Ghost. Acts 5:32 is set in the context of miraculous gifts. Verse 12 of this chapter states: "And by the hands of the apostles were many signs and wonders wrought among the people." It was this very fact that caused the high priest and those with him to be filled with indignation (v. 17) and to put the apostles in prison. That very night, by means of a miracle, the prison doors were opened and the apostles were sent to preach in the temple. Against this background, when Peter spoke of the "Holy Ghost, whom God hath given to them that obey him," and said that he (the Holy Ghost) was a witness with them (the apostles) of the truthfulness of the things they preached, he was obviously speaking of the fact that their testimony concerning Jesus was confirmed by the miracles they performed. The fact that they performed miracles showed they were obedient to God, for God gives the Holy Ghost only to them who obey him. The apostles gave testimony concerning the resurrection of Christ; the Holy Ghost corroborated their testimony by performing miracles through them. This is the very thing Jesus had said would happen. In speaking of the Holy Ghost which would proceed from the Father, Jesus said, "He shall testify of me." He then added, "And ye also shall bear witness, because ye have been with me from the beginning" (John 15:26, 27).

Conclusion

I see little possibility that any of the Christians to whom the books of the New Testament were originally written understood any mention of the Holy Ghost as being a reference to a non-miraculous indwelling. If one reads these books as if they were originally written to individuals and churches who already had a copy of the New Testament and who lived after miracles had ceased, then he will naturally think some of the references must be to a non-miraculous, personal indwelling, since miracles have ceased. But those of the first century would have no reason to think such.

Again I would emphasize that I believe the Holy Ghost dwells in Christians today, just as the Father and the Son dwell in us. But. I doubt this is what any of the writers of the New Testament books had in mind when they made reference to the Spirit's being in or being possessed by those Christians in the first century.

Whatever differences we may have over the subject of the Holy Spirit should not be allowed to alienate us from one another, so long as we are in agreement that there is no leadership or guidance of the Spirit other than that furnished by the written word.

It was my privilege to live only thirty miles from

the late beloved brother Gus Nichols the last seventeen years of his life. We differed over this matter, but our differences in no way hindered our fellowship. He preached in meetings and on other occasions at Adamsville where I lived and worked. I preached in the very last meeting the Sixth Avenue church in Jasper conducted while brother Nichols was still living. I attended meetings in which he preached at other places, and he attended meetings at other places where I was doing the preaching. He was a great source of encouragement to me. Our differences over this matter did not hinder our relationship at all. Though we differed, I knew brother Nichols was committed to being governed completely and totally by the word of God, and he knew the same about me. Though we differed in our understanding of this subject, what we tried to practice was the same. I would not pretend that I did as good a job in practicing it as did brother Nichols; few men have done so. Shortly before the death of brother Nichols a brother with whom I am largely in agreement on this particular subject wrote an article on the subject. In that article he called brother Nichols by name, left the impression he thought brother Nichols was a dangerous man, and even questioned the honesty of brother Nichols because of his position with reference to the Holy Spirit. This prompted me to write an article in which I pointed out that it is essential that we know who the enemies of the truth really are. Brother Nichols was not the enemy.

On the subject of the Holy Spirit, the enemy is the one who advocates some leadership of the Spirit in addition to that which is contained in the written word. Those committed to the written word as our only source of guidance, and yet who may differ with me on the subject of how the Spirit dwells in the Christian, are not the enemies.

VIEW 4: THE GIFT OR INDWELLING OF THE HOLY SPIRIT

Wayne Jackson
The Restorer (Vol. 7, No. 1, January 1987)

To a multitude assembled on the day of Pentecost the apostle Peter declared:

> *Repent ye, and be baptized every one of you in the name of Jesus Christ unto the remission of your sins; and ye shall receive the gift of the Holy Spirit (Acts 2:38).*

The identity of "the gift of the Holy Spirit," as that expression is used in Acts 2:38, has long been a matter of interesting discussion among Christians. Good and respected brethren hold differing viewpoints as to the meaning of the divine terminology employed in this passage. Aside from the radical notion that this verse asserts the perpetuity of miraculous gifts throughout the Christian age—an allegation which would clearly conflict with clear information elsewhere set forth in the New Testament (cf. 1 Cor. 13:8ff; Eph. 4:8ff)—there is room for honest disagreement among the Lord's people on this matter without there being any breach of fellowship.

The Views of Some Brethren

At the outset, I would like to briefly discuss several concepts which brethren hold regarding this matter which I believe to be incorrect.

Salvation. Some argue that the gift of the Holy Spirit mentioned in this passage is merely a reference to salvation from past sins. But this theory appears to gloss the very language of the verse. It seems very clear to this writer that "the gift of the Holy Spirit" is something *different from* and *in consequence of* the reception of the forgiveness of sins. Note the dual use of the conjunction "and" in this context: "Repent ye, and be baptized . . . unto the remission of your sins; and ye shall receive the gift of the Holy Spirit." If baptism is different from repentance, should not a similar recognition be given to the distinction between salvation and the gift of the Holy Spirit? Moreover, other passages also suggest that the reception of the Holy Spirit is a blessing given in consequence of salvation (cf. Gal. 4:6).

Miraculous gifts. Some contend that the gift of the Holy Spirit in Acts 2:38 was the reception of supernatural signs as bestowed by the apostles' hands. If such a view is correct, it would seem that a reasonable approach to the passage would suggest that all who were baptized that day (cf. 2:41) received not only forgiveness of sins, but also supernatural gifts, so that literally hundreds of disciples were subsequently performing miracles in the city of Jerusalem. This notion, however, suffers from the lack of any supporting evidence in the book of Acts. There is absolutely no indication, from Acts 2 through chapter 5, that anyone other than the apostles possessed miraculous gifts. Note the following: "and fear came upon every soul: and many wonders and signs were done *through the apostles"* (Acts 3:43). The miracle performed by Peter and John in Acts 3 seems to have been an unusual event. The Jewish leaders commented:

> *. . . for that indeed a notable miracle hath been wrought through them, is manifest to ail that dwell in Jerusalem; and we cannot deny it (Acts 4:16).*

There is no hint that multitudes of Christians were duplicating such signs in the city. Again:

> *And* ***by the hands of the apostles*** *were many signs and wonders wrought among the people; and they were all with one accord in Solomon's porch. But of the rest durst no man join himself to them: howbeit the people magnified them . . . (Acts 5:13).*

The religious awe with which the multitudes held the apostles suggests that they were doing signs not characteristic of the saints generally. It is only when one comes to Acts 6:6ff that mention is made of the imposition of the apostles' hands and the subsequent exercise of miraculous gifts by others (cf. Acts 6:8).

It has been suggested that the terms "gift" *(dorea)*

and "receive" *(lambano)* in Acts 2:38 indicate a miraculous phenomenon, and thus in this context denote the supernatural gifts made available through the laying on of the apostles' hands. That such is not a valid observation can be verified easily by the consultation of a Greek concordance. Compare, for example, *dorea* in John 4:10, Roman 5:15, 17, and *lambano* in John 12:48, Mark 10:30. Moreover, the fact is, the most common Greek term for those gifts conveyed by the imposition of apostolic hands is the word *charisma* (cf. Rom. 12:6; 1 Cor. 12:4, 9, 28, 30, 31; 1 Tim. 4:14; 2 Tim. 1:6).

It is alleged that Acts 2:38 is parallel with Mark 16:16ff in that both sections promise salvation and the reception of signs. I personally do not believe that the passages are either grammatically or contextually parallel in all respects. Mark 16:16ff contains a *general* declaration that miraculous gifts would accompany the body of believers, confirming their divinely given testimony, whereas the persons *directly addressed* in Acts 2:38 were promised both remission of sins and the gift of the Holy Spirit. It does not seem reasonable that they would have understood the promise to have been *unlimited* with reference to forgiveness, but *limited* in regard to the gift of the Spirit

The Word only. Other good brethren hold that "the gift of the Holy Spirit" is merely a metaphorical expression suggesting that only the Spirit's influence, by means of the inspired Word, indwells the Christian. In my opinion, this concept does not adequately explain all of the biblical data on this theme.

A frequent line of argument in support of this position is to assemble two lists of passages which show common effects produced by both the Spirit and the Word. This is, however, the fallacy of analogy. (Compare the typical Oneness Pentecostal argument whereby lists of similar traits relative to the Father and the Son are assembled in an attempt to prove that they are the same Person.) The fact that the Holy Spirit frequently uses the Word as his instrument (Eph. 6:17) does not speak to the issue of whether or not he indwells the child of God.

The "Word only" view seems to fall under the weight of the context of Acts 2 as a whole. For example, Peter's auditors on the day of Pentecost "gladly received his word" (v. 41), hence, the influence of the Spirit *before* their baptism. This is evidenced by their question, "What shall we do?" (v. 37), as well as an implied penitent disposition. Yet the promised Spirit was given after baptism. Since the Spirit operated on the Pentecostians through the Word prior to their baptism. Just what did they receive as a “gift" after their baptism?

The Author’s Viewpoint

The indwelling Spirit. It is the conviction of numerous highly esteemed brethren that the Holy Spirit, as a "gift,” is bestowed upon the obedient believer (Acts 2:38. 5:32, 1 Cor. 6:19, etc.), and is an indwelling presence in his life. Let us consider several facets of this matter.

According to Acts 2:38, the baptized believer is promised "the gift of the Holy Spirit." Is this a gift *consisting* of the Spirit, or a gift *given* by the Spirit? Actually, from a strictly grammatical viewpoint, it could be either. Some, though, have suggested that grammatically the phrase cannot refer to the Spirit as a gift. That simply is not correct. The expression *tou hagiou pneumatos* in Greek is in the genitive case. Greek grammar books list more than a dozen usages for the genitive (cf. J. Harold Greenlee. A *Concise Exegetical Grammar of New Testament Greek.* Eerdmans, 1963, pp. 28-31). It is context either in its narrower or broader sense that will determine the use of the genitive case in a given circumstance.

The fact of the matter is, almost every Greek authority known to this writer contends that the genitive of Acts 2:38 is epexegetical (appositional), i.e., *the Holy Spirit is the gift* (cf. the lexicons of: Arndt & Gingrich, 209. Thayer, 161; Robinson, 196; also the works of Kittel, II, 167; Vine, 147; Robertson, *Word Pictures.* III. 36; Moulton, Howard, Turner, *Grammar,* III, 214; *Expositor's Greek Testament.* II, 91). These sources are not cited as theological experts, but as language authorities; they obviously did not feel that it is grammatically *impossible* for the gift to consist of the Spirit himself. That "the gift of the Holy Spirit" can be the Spirit himself, and that usage be grammatically correct is demonstrated by a comparison of Acts 10:45 and 10:47, even though the respective contexts reveal that different "measures" of the Spirit are in view.

It is probably safe to say that most of the scholars within our restoration heritage have also argued this meaning of "the gift of the Holy Spirit" in Acts 2:38, even when differing on the nature of receiving the Spirit. J.W. McGarvey wrote: “The expression means the Holy Spirit as a gift, and the reference is to that indwelling of the Holy Spirit by which we bring forth the fruits of the Spirit, and without which we are not of Christ" *(New Commentary on Acts. I*, p. 39). Moses Lard said: "Certainly the gift of the Spirit is the Spirit itself given" *(Lard's Quarterly.* 11, p. 104, cf. also Lipscomb and Sewell, *Questions Answered* p. 318).

Supporting evidence. The most forceful argument for this viewpoint is the subsequent testimony of the New Testament regarding the reception of the Holy Spirit by the believer. Note the following.

1. In Acts 5:32 it is affirmed: “And we are witnesses of these things; and so is the Holy Spirit, whom God hath given to them that obey him.” Some would confine this passage to the apostles. Note, however, the "them" (others) who are mentioned in addition to the “we" (apostles).

2. Within the Roman letter. *In a context which discusses the indwelling Spirit* as a *possession of the saints* (cf. Rom. 8:9, 11, 16, 26, 27), the apostle Paul declares that the Holy Spirit and the human spirit bear dual witness to the fact that we are children of God (v. 16). Does our spirit actually dwell within us?

Some would suggest that only the Holy Spirit's influence through the Word is here considered. Notice, though, it is the indwelling Spirit *himself* who bears testimony with us (see also 8:26). Compare the language of John 4:2 where it is stated that while the Lord representatively baptized disciples, he "HIMSELF baptized not." There is a difference between what one does *himself* and what he accomplishes through an agent.

3. Paul inquired of the Corinthian saints: "Or know ye not that your body is the temple of the Holy Spirit which is in you, which ye have from God? and ye are not your own; for ye were bought with a price: glorify God therefore in your body" (1 Cor. 6:19). The Greek word for "temple" is *naos*, and it is an allusion to that holy sanctuary of the Mosaic economy wherein God actually made his presence known (cf. Ex. 25:22). Here is an interesting question: if the Holy Spirit bears a relationship to men today only "through the Word," and yet, admittedly, he influences the alien sinner through the Word, would it be proper to suggest that the sinner's body is "the temple of the Holy Spirit" to whatever extent he is affected by the Word?

4. Consider 1 Corinthians 12:13. "For in one Spirit (i.e., the Spirit's operation by means of the gospel) were we all baptized into one body . . . AND (an additional thought) were all made to drink of one Spirit" (1 Cor. 12:13). What is the difference in the Spirit's relationship to us *before* baptism and *after* it?

In Paul's dual references to the Spirit in this passage, is he suggesting the identical concept in both statements?

5. In Galatians 4:6 the Spirit is said to be sent into our hearts *because we are* (i.e., in consequence of being) sons of God. Would not this suggest a relationship that is different from the mere influence of the Word, since the sinner has the leading of the Word *before* he becomes a child of God?

6. Finally, if the relationship of the Holy Spirit is exactly the same to both sinner and saint (i.e., only through the Word), can it be affirmed that the sinner, to whatever extent that he is influenced by the Word, has the "earnest of the Spirit" (2 Cor. 1:22; 5:5; cf. Eph. 1:13, 14)? Do not these passages, and those above, set forth a precious promise that is exclusively confined to the Christian?

Some Points to Consider

Sincere brethren believe that there are strong arguments which negate the idea that the Spirit personally indwells the child of God. We will consider several of these.

1. It is argued that if the Holy Spirit actually dwelt in all Christians, he would be divided. If we may kindly say so, this a rather materialistic view of deity. The fact of the matter is, the apostles of Christ were filled with the Spirit of God (Acts 2:4), and yet the Spirit was still one (cf. 1 Cor. 12:9). It is countered, though, that the Holy Spirit actually did not dwell even in the apostles. Rather, it is alleged, the

Spirit was only with them in the sense that they were miraculously endowed with divine power. However, it must be noted that the apostles had the supernatural power of the Holy Spirit before the day of Pentecost (cf. Matt 10:8; 12:28). This is obviously what the Lord had in mind when he affirmed that the Spirit was "with" (para) those disciples; yet, additionally, the Savior promised, "he SHALL BE in (en) you ' (John 14:17). In view of this passage, how can it possibly be argued that the Holy Spirit cannot actually be in a person?

2. It has been suggested that if the Holy Spirit actually dwelt in someone that would be a form of "incarnation," hence, the person would be deity. This is an erroneous assumption. The Spirit was in the apostles (Acts 2:4), but they were not deity. Peter refused to be worshipped as though he were a divine being (Acts 10:26). In an incarnation, deity *becomes* flesh (cf. John 1:14), but such is not the case when the Spirit simply indwells the believer's body. When God called to Moses "out of the midst" of a bush (Ex. 3:4), that did not imply that the bush was divine.

3. Others would contend that if the Holy Spirit personally dwells in the Christian then he would be able to perform miracles. The connection is unwarranted. John the Baptist performed no miracles (John 10:41), and yet he was "filled with the Holy Spirit, even from his mother's womb" (Luke 1:15). Incidentally, the preposition "from" in this passage is the Greek term *ek* meaning from the inside to the outside,

thus suggesting that John was filled with the Spirit even *while in his mother's womb.* This certainly excludes the notion that the Holy Spirit can dwell in one only through the agency of the Word.

4. It is further argued that even though the Samaritans had been baptized (Acts 8:12), they had not received the Holy Spirit (8:16), hence, there is no indwelling of the Spirit at the point of baptism. This assertion, however, overlooks a very important phrase in verse 16. The text states: ". . . for as yet it was fallen upon none of them: *only they had been baptized into the name of the Lord Jesus."* Why did not the sentence conclude with the words, "as yet it was fallen upon none of them," if absolutely no reception of the Spirit was being affirmed? Certainly such would have been sufficient to complete that thought. Rather, though, a qualifying clause is added: "only (*monon de*—literally, 'but only') they had been baptized . . ." Thus, the sense likely is: ". . . for as yet it had fallen upon none of them: but only (in the sense bestowed when) they had been baptized into the name of the Lord Jesus." This compares well with the promise of the Spirit at the time of one's baptism "in the name of Jesus Christ" (Acts 2:38). Concerning Acts 8:16, McGarvey notes: ". . . previous to the arrival of Peter and John the Holy Spirit had fallen *with its miraculous powers* on none of the Samaritans" *(Ibid.,* p. 142. emphasis added).

5. It is contended that both God and Christ are

said to dwell in us, though they do not actually inhabit our bodies, so, similarly, is the case with the Spirit. However, we are expressly told that God dwells in us *by means of the Spirit.* Paul says the Ephesians were "a habitation of God in the Spirit" (Eph. 2:22), and John affirms: ". . . we know that he abideth in us, by the Spirit which he gave us"(1 John 3:24; cf. 4:13).

Benefits of the Spirit's indwelling

Many brethren believe that there are residual benefits to acknowledging the indwelling presence of the Holy Spirit in the life of the Christian. Let us consider a couple of these.

1. *The Confident Life* — Every child of God is painfully aware of his inability to live perfectly before his creator (cf. Rom. 7:14ff). Frequently, we have deep spiritual needs of which we are not even aware. We ought not to despair, however, for "the Spirit also helpeth our infirmity: for we know not how to pray as we ought; but the Spirit himself maketh intercession for us with groanings which cannot be uttered" (Rom. 6:26). There are several important truths affirmed in this passage: (a) We have needs which we do not adequately know how to address, (b) in this regard, the Spirit continually helps us (literally, constantly bears the load with us), (c) This assistance he "himself" (personally) provides, (d) He takes our unutterable groanings and, by his ongoing intercessory activity, conveys our needs to the Father, (e) God, who searches the hearts (where

the Spirit abides—Gal. 4:6), perceives the "mind of the Spirit" and responds to our needs consistent with his own will (cf. Rom. 8:27). What a thrilling concept of the Spirit's activity in our lives. Moses Lard has a wonderful discussion on this passage in his *Commentary on Romans,* pp. 276-278.

2. *Holiness*—The Greek world into which Christianity was born tended to deprecate the human body. There was a proverbial saying, "The body is a tomb." Epictetus said, "I am a poor soul shackled to a corpse." That concept accommodated a fleshly mode of living. Since only the soul was important and not the body, one could give himself wantonly to the indulgences of the flesh. It is this factor that certainly lies behind Paul's rebuke of carnal indulgence in the church at Corinth. The body is not to be given over to fornication (1 Cor. 6:13ff). One of the apostle's effective arguments for the sanctity of the Christian's body is that the Holy Spirit indwells that body as the temple of God, hence, those saints were to glorify the Father in their bodies (1 Cor. 6:19, 20).

We are confident that an awareness of the Spirit's abiding presence can be a powerful motivation to godly living. J. D. Thomas has noted that the doctrine "of the personal indwelling of the Spirit and a strong providential activity aids our own spiritual development towards its highest potential. Though the age of miracles is over, spiritual relationships and spiritual activities are not over! The awareness that the third member of the Godhead personally and actually dwells within us is a tremendous incentive to holiness" (The *Spirit and Spirituality.* Biblical Research Press, 1962, p. 52).

Conclusion

In affirming that the Holy Spirit dwells within the child of God, one need not suggest (a) that miracles are performed today, (b) that the Spirit "guides" or "illuminates" us in some way apart from the Scriptures, (c) that he operates directly upon the saint's heart, etc. The fact of the Spirit's indwelling is a different issue altogether from the various modes of his operation, as such were effected in the apostolic age.

I personally believe that a word of caution is in order as to the manner in which this controversy is addressed in our speaking and writing. Though most brethren acknowledge that this particular issue is not a matter of "fellowship," some, when addressing viewpoints that differ from their own, do so in a very condescending and caustic fashion. We do not believe that such a disposition is in the interest of candid investigation. Let us approach subjects of this type with a spirit of mutual respect and kindly accord.

"BE FILLED WITH THE SPIRIT"

Don Deffenbaugh

INTRODUCTION

"Be filled with the Spirit" is the magical expression of our day. It is being echoed in the four corners of the earth. By it, people mean that they have been baptized in the Spirit. By it, some Christians believe that they have a direct indwelling of the Spirit which enables them to be super-spiritual, and to enjoy unbelievable and unexplainable experiences.

It is a Biblical expression that is not only misunderstood by those in the classical Pentecostal and charismatic movements, but it is also misunderstood by many in the church of our Lord. What does the Bible mean when this expression is used?

Passages in Which the Expression is Found

No intelligent conclusions can be drawn concerning the expression until one has looked at the passages using it.

(1) Our *first list* of passages is where the word "Spirit" is used in connection with *pimplemi (pletho),* meaning "to fill:" Lk. 1:15, Lk. 1:41, Lk. 1:67, Acts 2:4, Acts 4:8, Acts 4:31, Acts 9:17, and Acts 13:9.

(2) *Our second list* is of passages where the word "Spirit" is used in connection with *pleroo,* meaning

"to fill:" Acts 13:52 and Eph. 5:18.

(3) *Our third list* contains passages where the word "Spirit" is used in connection with *pleres,* meaning "full of:" Lk. 4:1, Acts 6:3, Acts 6:5, Acts 7:55, Acts 11:24.

A Study of Each Passage Involving "Pimplemi"

(1) Luke 1:15. The first passage we find in the New Testament using this expression where *pimplemi* is involved is Lk. 1:15. The angel in announcing to Zacharias the birth of John observed that "he will be filled with the Holy Spirit, while yet in his mother's womb." Because it is obvious that in every other case in the New Testament where Spirit is used in connection with *pimplemi* that it is miraculous, we thus conclude that such is the case with this passage. With this conclusion J.S. Lamar agrees when he says that this is a Hebrew hyperbole denoting that John was to be filled with the Holy Spirit "from the earliest period."[1] Barnes holds the view, "Shall be divinely designated or appointed to this office and qualified for it by all needful communications from the Holy Spirit."[2]

(2) Lk. 1:41 is our second passage. There is no question but that this is a miraculous filling with the Holy Spirit, especially when one views the results,

---

[1] J. S. Lamar, *Commentary on Luke*, p. 23.

[2] Albert. Barnes, *Barnes on the New Testament, Luke — John*, p. 4.

"She cried out with a loud voice . . ." (vs. 42-45).

(3) Lk. 1:67 refers to Zacharias being filled with the Holy Spirit and the result was that he prophesied; hence, we are dealing with another case of the miraculous.

(4) In Acts 2:4, Luke refers to the apostles being baptized in the Holy Spirit in the following manner, "And they were all filled with the Holy Spirit and began to speak with other tongues, as the Spirit gave them utterance." It is quite obvious that we are dealing with the miraculous in this passage.

(5) In Acts 4:8, when Peter was filled with the Holy Spirit, he did some inspired preaching (vs. 8-12). Again, we are dealing with the miraculous.

(6) Acts 4:31. When the companions of Peter and John heard what the chief priests and the elders had said unto them they prayed and "they were all filled with the Holy Spirit . . ." and the result was that they began to speak the word of God with boldness (Acts 4:31). This sounds like inspired preaching to me.

(7) Acts 9:17 presents some difficulties to us, but they are the kind of difficulties that can be settled by a careful study of the text and its context. Saul was to become Paul, the apostle, and as an apostle he had to be baptized in the Holy Spirit. It is quite obvious that he possessed this measure of the Spirit (2 Cor. 12:11), yet only Christ could administer Holy Spirit baptism (Matt 3:11). The reason why it is mentioned in connection with the coming of Ananias is that if

Saul had refused to listen to Ananias, he would neither have received his sight nor have been baptized in the Holy Spirit. Even though Ananias did not give the Spirit to Saul, he would not have received it but for Ananias' coming. It is most significant for us to note that Saul's being filled with the Spirit is not attributed to the laying on of Ananias' hands. What did result from the laying on of his hands was that Saul received his sight (vs. 13, 18). We are again dealing with the miraculous.

(8) Acts 13:9 is yet another miraculous filling. The result is a miracle of judgment. Elymas the sorcerer was struck blind for a season because he withstood Paul and Barnabas as they worked with Sergius Paulus who desired to hear the word of Gad.

When "Spirit" is used in connection with this word there is evidently a reference to the miraculous.

A Study of Passages Involving "Pleroo"

(1) In Acts 13:52 we have a reference to the non-miraculous. There are at least three reasons why we have reached this conclusion in reference to this verse. (a) The verb form shows a continued action, "continually filled." (b) "Spirit" appears in connection with "joy" which is non-miraculous. (c) There is every indication that all the disciples were filled with the Spirit, yet not all disciples had the miraculous measure of the Spirit.

(2) When one studies Eph. 5:18-19 along with the companion passage, Col. 3:16, he must be convinced at once that we are dealing with the non-miraculous.

The fact that *all* Christians are to be thus filled, is proof that we are dealing with the non-miraculous. Again, not all New Testament Christians were miraculously endowed. In this passage we are dealing with a command, ". . . be filled with the Spirit." There is no command to be miraculously filled with the Holy Spirit in all the New Testament, unless of course, this is a case in point. But, it must be remembered that the miraculous measure of the Spirit lies in the realm of promise and not command.

When "Spirit" is used in connection with this word there is a reference to the non-miraculous.

A Study of Each Passage Involving "Pleres"

(1) In Lk. 4:1 we find the expression, and it must be remembered that it is used in reference to Christ immediately following the coming of the Holy Spirit upon him at his baptism (Lk. 3:22). McGarvey says, "Just after his baptism, with the glow of the descended Spirit still upon him, and the commending voice of the Father still ringing in his ears, Jesus is rushed into the suffering of temptation."[3] It must be remembered in this connection that according to John, our Lord had the Spirit without measure (Jn. 3:34).

(2) Acts 6:3, 5. Acts 6:3 is a passage which tells of the qualifications of those men who were to serve

---

[3] J.W. McGarvey, *The Four-fold Gospel — Matthew, Mark, Luke, John*, p. 87.

tables. The expression in this passage appears to refer to the non-miraculous. One reason for concluding such is that it is included with other qualifications that are non-miraculous, "of good report" and "full of wisdom." Even though some of these men were able to work miracles at a later date (Acts 8), such is no real proof that they were able to do it at this time. As a matter of fact, at this point in the history of New Testament church the only ones of record who could perform the miraculous were the apostles. McGarvey's observation is, "He means men who were full of the Spirit as respects the fruits of a holy life."[4]

Acts 6:5 merely shows that the multitude chose Stephen, a man who possessed the qualifications set forth in Acts 6:3. We are not to conclude that the others did not possess these same qualifications. Verse 6 of this reading offers us some difficulty. The passage refers to the laying on of the apostles' hands. There are at least three possible meanings: (a) that the apostles imparted to them the *gifts* measure of the Spirit; (b) that the apostles were merely setting them apart to this special function; (c) that the apostles were doing both; imparting the *gifts* measure of the Spirit and setting them apart to this special function. My choice is the last of the three. I believe that both ideas are involved. You see, Philip possessed the miraculous measure of the Spirit (Acts 8); and, if Acts

---

[4] J.W. McGarvey, *New Commentary on Acts of Apostles*, p. 105.

6:6 does not refer, at least in part, to the *gifts* measure, then we have no New Testament account of Philip receiving the same. Furthermore, as far as we know, there was as yet no elders in the New Testament church; and, hence, the apostles were leading the congregation and would be the ones to set these men apart to the function.

(3) Acts 7:55. When Stephen was filled with the Holy Spirit he was able to look up into heaven and see the glory of God (Acts 7:55). The results of his being filled with the Holy Spirit show us that this is a reference to the miraculous.

(4) Acts 11:24 seems to be a parallel to Acts 6:3, 5. Again, because of its association with faith, it appears to be a non-miraculous filling; and, hence, is a reference to Barnabas being full of the Spirit as respects the fruits of a holy life (Gal. 5:22-23).

The result of being "filled with the Spirit" is to be "full of the Spirit." There are times in the New Testament when to be "full of the Spirit" refers to the miraculous, and there are other times when it refers to the non-miraculous.

Deductions to be Drawn from This Study

(1) *First,* there was a period of time in the New Testament church when to "be filled with the Spirit" meant that they were given miraculous abilities: Acts 2:4, Acts 4:8, Acts 4:31, Acts 9:17, Acts 13:9, Acts 7:55.

(2) *Secondly,* during that same period of time, to "be filled with the Spirit" meant that they were to be

of distinguished piety: Acts 6:3, Acts 6:5, Acts 11:24, Acts 13:52, Eph. 5:18.

(3) *Thirdly,* it is therefore erroneous for our classical Pentecostal and charismatic friends to conclude that the expression "be filled with the Spirit" is equal to Holy Spirit baptism. There are only two cases of Holy Spirit baptism in the New Testament (Acts 2, 10, 11) and these fulfill the prophecy of Joel 2:28-29. The last recorded case of Holy Spirit baptism was in A.D. 41, the first case in A.D. 33. Paul said in A.D. 64, "there is one baptism." By the time Paul wrote Eph. 4:5 the baptism of the Holy Spirit had served its purpose in (a) guiding and qualifying the apostles, and (b) confirming the fact that the gospel was for the Gentiles as well as the Jews. There is one baptism for today and that is baptism in water for the remission of sins (Acts 2:38).

(4) *Fourthly,* in those cases of non-miraculous filling of the Spirit in the New Testament, there is no proof of super piety, better-felt-than-told feeling, fantastic highs, etc.; but, rather, that these disciples were producing the fruit of the Spirit in their lives. As Barnes says, they were of "distinguished piety."[5]

(5) *Fifthly,* there is *NO* possibility that today's Christian can be filled with the Spirit in a miraculous manner. There are two reasons why this is so: (a) Holy Spirit baptism has been fulfilled (Acts 2, 10, 11), and (b) there can be no laying on of the apostles'

---

[5] Albert. Barnes, *Barnes on the New Testament*, Acts, p. 111.

hands today (Acts 8:14-19).

CONCLUSION

May the Lord help us to be filled with the Spirit (Eph. 5:18)! But may the Lord also hasten the day when his people rely wholly upon the sword of the Spirit (Eph. 6:17) to lead, guide and direct them. When one follows the complete guide, his spiritual life will be complete, and he will be completely furnished unto every good work (2 Tim. 3:16-17). Only the evil and carnally minded look for direct operations of the Spirit which serve as their signs (Matt. 12 39).

Powers by Baptism of the Holy Spirit?

Clem Thurman
Gospel Minutes (Vol. 70, No. 8, Feb. 19, 2021)

> "Dear brothers: if, in Acts 10, Cornelius and his household received the same measure of the Holy Spirit as did the apostles on the Day of Pentecost, would they have been able to perform all the miraculous evidences as did the apostles? -C.S., TX"

Peter described his preaching to Cornelius when he got back among his Jewish brothers.

> *"And as I began to speak, the Holy Spirit fell on them, even as on us at the beginning. And I remembered the word of the Lord, how he said, John indeed baptized with water; but ye shall be baptized in the Holy Spirit. If then God gave unto them the like gift as he did also unto us, when we believed on the Lord Jesus Christ, who was I, that I could withstand God?" (Acts 11:15-17).*

Two points are clear from this passage. First, Cornelius and his household received *"the like gift"* as the apostles had received on Pentecost. Second, this event caused Peter to remember the Lord's promise concerning being baptized by the Holy

Spirit. Thus, it seems clear that Cornelius and his household received the baptism of the Holy Spirit as had the apostles.

Paul wrote about *"gifts of the Holy Spirit"* (all of which were miraculous) in 1 Corinthians 12:1-11. And, the principles he set forth are important to understanding the miraculous working of the Holy Spirit. *"Now there are diversities of gifts, but the same Spirit"* (1 Cor. 12:4). This verse shows that the Spirit did not empower every person to do the same thing. One might prophesy, another might speak in tongues, and another might work miracles. The fact that the person was given one of these gifts did not mean he was given another gift of the Spirit. *"And there are diversities of workings, but the same God, who worketh all things in all"* (1 Cor. 12:6) demonstrates that it was God who determined what power was to be used, and when and how. The one who was given miraculous power could not "turn it off" at his discretion. God controlled these gifts. *"But to each one is given the manifestation of the Spirit to profit withal"* (1 Cor. 12:7). This verse means that the power was not to benefit the one who received it. This is a very important point. Modem day "miracle workers" are searching for something that will benefit them. But, the gifts of the Holy Spirit were never designed to benefit the person who received the gift, they were to enable that person to minister to others. After the apostle has listed nine *"gifts of the Holy Spirit"* (1 Cor. 12:8-10), he then states, *"But all these worketh the one and the same Spirit, dividing to each one severally even as he will"* (1 Cor. 12:11). In other words, God determined who received what spiritual gift and what it was to be used for.

Even though Paul was speaking of the *"gifts of the Holy Spirit"* in I Corinthians 12, the principles surely apply to the baptism of the Holy Spirit and powers that resulted from it. How many gifts did each of the apostles have? I assume they had, at various times, all of the gifts, but that is just an assumption. But, it is clear that their use of any miraculous power of the Holy Spirit would depend upon the need at that time, and even then God would determine whether it was to be used. This example is clear. Paul could heal the sick (Acts 14:8-10), cast out evil spirits (Acts 16:16-18) and even raise the dead (Acts 20:9-12). But, when a beloved companion became ill, Paul did not heal him. *"Erastus remained at Corinth: but Trophimus I left at Miletus sick"* (2 Tim. 4:20). Paul could not decide on his use of miraculous power, God did that for him. The purpose of all these miraculous gifts was to reveal and confirm the will of God to man (Mark 16:20; Heb. 2:3-4; 1 Cor. 2:9-13), and if a miracle did not serve that purpose, it was not done.

When the apostles were baptized with the Holy Spirit (Acts 1:4-5, 2:1-4), it was to enable them to know and preach the gospel.

> *"Ye shall receive power, when the Holy Spirit is come upon you: and ye shall be my*

witnesses both in Jerusalem, and in all Judaea and Samaria, and unto the uttermost part of the earth" (Acts 1:8).

Whatever miraculous measures were needed for that, God supplied through the Holy Spirit. When Cornelius was baptized with Holy Spirit (Acts 10:44-48), the situation was different. Cornelius didn't receive the Spirit to enable him to do the work which the apostles were doing, but to convince the Jewish Christians the Gentiles were to be equal heirs with them in the gospel. We know that is true, because that is the precise use which was made of the event. *"Can any man forbid the water, that these should not be baptized, who have received the Holy Spirit as well as we?"* (Acts 10:47).

Peter later recounted these events for the Jewish Christians back in Jerusalem. *"And when they heard these things, they held their peace, and glorified God, saying, Then to the Gentiles also hath God granted repentance unto life"* (Acts 11:18). When Paul healed the man at. Lystra, it caused the people to want to hear what he preached. That was the purpose of the miracle.

When Cornelius and his household *"spoke with tongues, and magnify God"* (Acts 10:46), it caused the Jewish Christians to accept the Gentiles, as *"that the Gentiles are fellow-heirs, and fellow-members of the body, and fellow-partakers of the promise in Christ Jesus through the gospel"* (Eph. 3:6). That was the purpose of that miracle. I find no evidence that Cornelius ever did another miraculous thing, neither can I find one reason in Scripture why he would be given such power after this one event. The point, then, is simple. The apostles were given such miraculous power as God determined they needed. And, He gave such power when, and how, He determined. Cornelius and his household *"spoke with tongues,"* but there is no indication that any of them ever had any other miraculous gift or were ever given this particular gift again. The fact that Cornelius was baptized with the Holy Spirit, just as the apostles were, did not mean he had equal power with them. As God determined what gift was given and to whom it was given, God also determined when and how that power was used.

TWENTY-FIVE POINTS, PLUS SIX MORE

Foy E. Wallace, Jr. Mission and Medium of the Holy Spirit.

The fact that every effect and influence that the Holy Spirit exerts upon and within us is affirmed of the Word of God proves that the Spirit operates only through the Word—that every effect or emotion that the Holy Spirit generates within us, the Word of God engenders.

1. The spiritual *begetting* is with the Word.

> *"Of his own will begat he us with the word of truth, that we should be a kind of first-fruits of his creatures"—Jas. 1:18.*
>
> *"For though ye have ten thousand instructors in Christ, yet have ye not many fathers: for in Christ. Jesus I have begotten you through the gospel"—1 Cor. 4:15.*

All life is generated through *seed.* When the Word—the spiritual seed—is planted in the heart, it germinates. The Word has in it the embryo of spiritual life.

2. The spiritual *birth* springs from the incorruptible and eternal Word.

> *"Being born again, not of corruptible*

> *seed, but of incorruptible, by the word of God, which liveth and abideth forever"—1 Pet. 1:23.*

3. The *quickening* of the heart is with the operation of the Word.

> *"And you hath he quickened, who were dead in trespasses and sins... even when we were dead in sins, hath quickened [made alive] us together with Christ, by grace are ye saved"—Eph. 2:1, 5.*
>
> *"Thy word hath quickened me... I will never forget thy precepts: for with them thou hast quickened me"—Psa. 119:50, 93.*
>
> *"Buried with him in baptism, wherein also ye are risen with him through the faith of the operation of God, who hath raised him from the dead. And you, being dead in your sins... hath he quickened together with him, having forgiven you all trespasses."—Col. 2:12-13*
>
> *"For the grace of God that bringeth salvation hath appeared to all men, Teaching us that, denying ungodliness and worldly lusts, we should live soberly, righteously, and godly, in this present world."—Titus 2:11-12.*

4. The spiritual *cleansing* is a process of the Word.

> *"Now ye are clean through the word that I have spoken unto you"—John 15:2.*
>
> *"Even as Christ also loved the church, and gave himself up for it; that he might sanctify and cleanse it with the washing of water by the word"—Eph. 5:26.*

5. The soul is *purified* in obedience to the Word.

> *"Seeing ye have purified your souls in obeying the truth through the Spirit unto unfeigned love of the brethren, see that ye love one another with a pure heart fervently"—1 Peter 1:22.*

6. The soul is *saved* by the implanted Word.

> *"Receive with meekness the engrafted word, which is able to save your souls. But be ye doers of the word, and not hearers only"—Jas. 1:21-22.*

7. The *justification* by faith comes through obedience to the Word.

> *"For not the hearers of the law are just before God, but the doers of the law shall be justified"—Rom. 2:13.*
>
> *Where is boasting then? It is excluded. By what law? of works? Nay: but by the law of faith.—Rom. 3:27*

And such were some of you: but ye are washed, but ye are sanctified, but ye are justified in the name of the Lord Jesus, and by the Spirit of our God.—1 Cor. 6:11

8. It was the apostle's desire for all to be *filled* with knowledge.

"That ye might be filled with the knowledge of his will in all wisdom and spiritual understanding"—Col. 1:9.

It was "through the power of the Holy Spirit—Rom. 15:13—that the knowledge of his will had come for the source of spiritual understanding.

9. The members of the church were given inspired instruction to let the *Word* dwell in them.

"Let the word of Christ dwell in you richly in all wisdom; teaching and admonishing one another in psalms and hymns and spiritual songs, singing with grace in your hearts to the Lord."—Col. 3:16.

The parallel passage is Eph. 5:18-19:

"Be filled with the Spirit, speaking to yourselves in psalms and hymns and spiritual songs, singing and making melody in your heart to the Lord."

10. The means of direction and guidance is that of being *led* by the Word.

> *"Thou shalt guide me with thy counsel, and afterward receive me to glory"—Psa. 73:24.*

> *"Thy word is a lamp unto my feet, and a light unto my pathway"—Psa. 119:105.*

> *"To give knowledge of salvation unto his people... to give light to them that sit in darkness... to guide our feet in the way of peace"—Luke 1:77-79.*

All who are guided by the Word are led by the Spirit.

11. The *witness* within the heart of true believers is the Word of Truth.

> *"And it is the Spirit that beareth witness, because the Spirit is truth"—1 John 5:6.*

12. The *growth* of the spiritual babe is by the milk of the Word.

> *"As newborn babes desire the sincere milk of the Word, that ye may grow thereby"—1 Pet. 2:1.*

The *sincere milk* means the pure unadulterated Word; and *grow thereby* means that the Word is all-sufficient to accomplish the end of spiritual growth.

13. The effectual *working* within is accomplished by the indwelling Word.

> *"For this cause also thank we God without ceasing, because, when ye received the word of God which ye heard of us, ye received it not as the word of men, but, as it is in truth, the word of God, which effectually worketh also in you that believe"—1 Thess. 2:13.*

14. The truth within produces *fruit* without.

> *"For the hope which is laid up for you in heaven, whereof ye heard before in the word of the truth of the gospel; which is come unto you... and bringeth forth fruit, as it doth also in you since the day ye heard of it, and knew the grace of God in truth"—Col. 1:5-6.*

15. The indwelling truth is the rule by which the followers of Christ *walk* in the doing of his entire will.

> *"I rejoice greatly that I found of thy children walking in truth, as we have received commandment from the Father... This is the commandment, that, as ye have heard from the beginning, ye should walk in it"—2 John 4.*
>
> *"I have no greater joy than to hear that my children walk in truth"—3 John 4.*

> *"Nevertheless, whereto ye have already attained, let us walk by the same rule, let us mind the same things"—Phil. 3: 16.*

There could be no better way of walking in the Spirit than to *walk in the truth.* It is the revelation of the Holy Spirit, and with this word of the Spirit to lead us, we may all with one mind walk by the same rulo.

16: The source of *strength* is the knowledge of the Word of His grace.

> *"And now, brethren, I commend you to God, and to the word of his grace, which is able to build you up, and to give you an inheritance among all them which are sanctified"—Acts 20:32.*

> *"That ye may be filled with the knowledge of his will... increasing in the knowledge of God; strengthened with all might, according to his glorious power"—Col. 1:10-11.*

> *"And I myself also am persuaded of you, my brethren, that ye also are full of goodness, filled with all knowledge, and able to admonish one another."—Rom. 15:14.*

17. The inspired Word has in it the power to *comfort* the bereaved.

> *"Wherefore comfort one another with these words"—1 Thess. 4:18.*

"And sent. Timothy, our brother, and minister of the gospel of Christ, to establish you, and to comfort you concerning your faith"—1 Thess. 3:2.

"For whatsoever things were written aforetime were written for our learning, that we through patience and comfort of the scriptures might have hope"—Rom. 15:4.

18. The spirit of *grace* in the apostolic epistles is set forth as the gospel of Christ.

"The ministry which I have received of the Lord Jesus, to testify the gospel of the grace of God... and to the word of his grace, which is able to build you up"—Acts 20:24, 34.

"The grace of God which bringeth salvation, teaching us"—Tit. 2:11-12.

"Who hath trodden underfoot the Son of God, and hath counted the blood of the covenant, wherewith he was sanctified, an unholy thing, and hath done despite unto the Spirit of grace"—Heb. 10:29.

19. The love of God is *shed* abroad in our hearts by the gospel.

"Lest the light of the glorious gospel of Christ should shine unto the;, for God who commanded light to shine out of darkness,

> *hath shined in our h*earts, to give the light of the knowledge of the glory of God in the face of Jesus Christ"—2 Cor. *4:4-6.*

The statement of Rom. 5:5, that the love of God is *shed* in our hearts by the Holy Spirit, and the statement of 2 Cor. 4:4-6 that the light of the knowledge of God is *shined* in our hearts by the gospel, have the same connotation.

20. The Word is said to *live* within the one who believes it.

> *"I am the bread of life: he that cometh to me shall never hunger.... I am the living bread which came down out of heaven: if any man eat this bread, he shall live forever"—John 6:35, 51.*

In the context between these two verses is the statement: "Every man therefore that hath heard, and hath learned of the Father, cometh unto me"—verse 45. The bread of life is received through being *taught,* and by having *heard,* and by *learning,* and thus through the bread of the *word,* its life is in us.

21. The Words spoken by Christ engender *spirituality* in us.

> *"It is the Spirit that quickeneth; the flesh profiteth nothing: the words that I speak unto you, they are spirit and they are life"—John 6:63.*

22. The Word within the heart *flows* outward into the life.

> *"But whosoever drinketh of the water that I shall give him shall never thirst; but the water that I shall give him shall be in him a well of water springing up into everlasting life."—John 4:14.*

> *"Our fathers did eat manna in the desert; as it is written, He gave them bread from heaven to eat... I am the bread of life: he that cometh to me shall never hunger; and he that believeth on me shall never thirst"—John 6:31, 35.*

> *"And did all eat the same spiritual meat; and did all drink the same spiritual drink; for they drank of that spiritual Rock that followed them: and that Rock was Christ"—1 Cor. 10:3-4.*

> *"How sweet are thy words to my taste! Yea, sweeter than honey to my mouth!"—Psa. 119:103.*

23. The entrance of the Word *enlightens* the heart.

> *"The entrance of thy words giveth light; it giveth understanding to the simple"—Psa. 119:130.*

> *"The statutes of the Lord are right, rejoicing the heart; the commandment of the*

> *Lord is pure, enlightening the eyes"—Psa. 19:8.*

24. The source of *understanding* is the inspiration of the Word.

> *"But there is a spirit in man: and the inspiration of the Almighty giveth them understanding"—Job 32:8.*
>
> *"Through thy precepts I get understanding: therefore I hate every false way"—Psa. 119:104.*
>
> *"All scripture is given by inspiration, and is profitable for doctrine, for reproof, for correction, for instruction in righteousness: that the man of God may be perfect, throughly furnished unto all good works"—2 Tim. 3:16-17.*

25. The work of *sanctification* is completed by the Word.

> *"Sanctify them through thy truth: thy word is truth"—John 1:17.*
>
> *"That he might sanctify and cleanse it with the washing of water by the word."—Eph. 5:26*

26. Not lending ear to the word is *resisting* the Spirit.

> *"Ye stiffnecked and uncircumcised in heart and ears, ye do always resist the Holy*

Spirit; as your fathers did, so do ye"—Acts 7:51.

"Yet many years didst thou forbear them, and testified against them by thy spirit in thy prophets: yet would they not give ear"—Neh. 9:30.

27. The unbelief of the Word is *grieving* the Spirit.

"Today if ye will hear his voice, harden not your heart... as in the provocation... forty years long was I grieved with this generation, and said, It is a people that do err in their heart, and they have not known my ways"—Psa. 95: 7-10.

"Wherefore the Holy Spirit saith, Today if you will hear his voice, harden not your hearts, as in the provocation... wherefore I was grieved with that generation... Take heed, brethren, lest there be in any one of you an evil heart of unbelief, in departing from the living God"—Heb. 3:7-12.

28. The disobedience to the Word is *quenching* the Spirit.

"Quench not the Spirit—l Thess. 5:19.

29. Speaking against the Word is *blaspheming* the Spirit.

"But when the Jews saw the multitudes,

they were filled with envy, and spake against those things which were spoken by Paul, contradicting and blaspheming"—Acts 13:45.

"All sins shall be forgiven unto the sons of men, and blasphemies wherewith soever they shall blaspheme: but he that shall blaspheme against the Holy Spirit hath never forgiveness, but is in danger of eternal damnation."—Mark 3:28-29

"That the name of God and his doctrine be not blasphemed"—1 Tim. 6:1

30. The body that is interred in the tomb will be *raised* at the last day by the Word of Christ.

"For the hour is coming, in the which all that are in the graves shall hear his voice, and shall come forth; they that have done good, unto the resurrection of life; and they that have done evil, unto the resurrection of damnation"—John 5:28-29.

"The Lord himself shall descend with a shout, with the voice of the archangel, and with the trump of God."—1 Thess. 4:16

"In a moment, in the twinkling of an eye, at the last trump: for the trumpet shall sound, and the dead shall be raised incorruptible, and we shall be changed."—1 Cor. 15:52

31. The criterion of the *judgment* will be the Word of Christ.

> *"And if any man hear my words, and believe not, I judge him not: for I came not to judge the world, but to save the world. He that rejecteth me, and receiveth not my words, hath one that judgeth him: the word that I have spoken, the same shall judge him in the last day"—John 12:47-48.*

Now, there are the twenty-five items, with six more for good measure, in the positive proof that *every effect and emotion that the Holy Spirit produces, the Word of God engenders.*

The Holy Spirit operates through the word, not by direct operation!

Made in the USA
Monee, IL
19 May 2021